A-level Religious Studies

ISLAM

Waqar Ahmad Ahmedi

HODDER
EDUCATION
AN HACHETTE UK COMPANY

Acknowledgements

Extracts from the Qur'an: *The Qur'an* A new translation by M. A. S. Abdel Haleem
© M. A. S. Abdel Haleem 2004, 2005, reprinted with amends 2008, Oxford University
Press. Reproduced with permission of the Licensor through PLSclear.

Every effort has been made to trace all copyright holders, but if any have been
inadvertently overlooked, the Publishers will be pleased to make the necessary
arrangements at the first opportunity.

Although every effort has been made to ensure that website addresses are correct at
time of going to press, Hodder Education cannot be held responsible for the content of
any website mentioned in this book. It is sometimes possible to find a relocated web
page by typing in the address of the home page for a website in the URL window of
your browser.

Hachette UK's policy is to use papers that are natural, renewable and recyclable
products and made from wood grown in well-managed forests and other controlled
sources. The logging and manufacturing processes are expected to conform to the
environmental regulations of the country of origin.

Orders: please contact Hachette UK Distribution, Hely Hutchinson Centre,
Milton Road, Didcot, Oxfordshire, OX11 7HH. Telephone: +44 (0)1235 827827.
Email education@hachette.co.uk Lines are open from 9 a.m. to 5 p.m., Monday
to Friday. You can also order through our website: www.hoddereducation.co.uk

ISBN: 978 1 3983 1716 1

© Waqar Ahmad Ahmedi 2021

First published in 2021 by
Hodder Education,
An Hachette UK Company
Carmelite House
50 Victoria Embankment
London EC4Y 0DZ

www.hoddereducation.co.uk

Impression number   10 9 8 7 6 5 4 3 2 1

Year   2025 2024 2023 2022 2021

Cover photo – Aviator70 – stock.adobe.com

Illustrations by Integra Software Services

Typeset in India

Printed in Spain

A catalogue record for this title is available from the British Library.

My Revision Planner

REVISED   TESTED   EXAM READY

A-level Religious Studies: Islam

My Revision Planner

Suggested answer guidance to exam practice at **www.hoddereducation.co.uk/myrevisionnotesdownloads**

Specification mapping grid

Topics	AQA AS	AQA A	Eduqas AS	Eduqas A	OCR AS	OCR A	Pearson Edexcel AS	Pearson Edexcel A	WJEC AS	WJEC A
1 Islam: context and need										
Jahiliyya			✓	✓					✓	✓
The need for revelation			✓	✓					✓	✓
2 Life and teachings of Prophet Muhammad										
Birth, childhood and early life			✓	✓			✓	✓	✓	✓
The Night of Power (610ᴄᴇ)			✓	✓			✓	✓	✓	✓
Further revelations and growth of Islam (610–621ᴄᴇ)			✓	✓			✓	✓	✓	✓
Hijrah and the establishment of Islam in Madinah (622ᴄᴇ)			✓	✓			✓	✓	✓	✓
3 Sources of authority and shari`a										
What is shari`a?			✓	✓	✓		✓	✓		✓
What is the Qur'an?	✓	✓	✓	✓	✓	✓	✓	✓	✓	✓
The revelation and compilation of the Qur'an	✓	✓	✓	✓	✓	✓	✓	✓	✓	✓
The treatment of the Qur'an			✓	✓	✓	✓			✓	✓
What are the Sunnah and Hadith?	✓	✓	✓	✓	✓	✓	✓	✓	✓	✓
Ijma', qiyas, ijtihad			✓	✓	✓					✓
4 Beliefs and concepts: articles (Sunni) and roots of faith (Shi'a)										
The six articles of faith (Sunni) and five roots of Usul al-Din (Shi'a)							✓	✓		
Allah	✓	✓	✓	✓	✓	✓	✓	✓	✓	✓
Angels			✓	✓	✓	✓	✓	✓	✓	✓
Revelation (wahy) and the role and nature of prophets			✓	✓	✓	✓	✓	✓		✓
Nabi and rasul			✓	✓	✓	✓	✓	✓		✓
Islam and other Abrahamic faiths			✓	✓	✓	✓	✓	✓		✓
The Prophet Muhammad	✓	✓	✓	✓	✓	✓	✓	✓		✓
What is the Imamah?	✓	✓			✓	✓	✓	✓		
Resurrection and afterlife	✓	✓	✓	✓	✓	✓	✓	✓	✓	✓
Divine decree and free will	✓	✓			✓	✓	✓	✓		
5 Practices and identity										
The foundations of Islam: Five Pillars (Sunni) and Ten Obligatory Acts (Shi'a)	✓	✓					✓	✓		
Shahadah	✓	✓	✓	✓			✓	✓		
Salah, worship and other forms of prayer	✓	✓	✓	✓			✓	✓	✓	✓
The mosque (masjid)	✓	✓	✓	✓					✓	✓
Charitable giving	✓	✓	✓	✓			✓	✓	✓	✓
Hajj	✓	✓	✓	✓			✓	✓	✓	✓
Sawm and Ramadan	✓	✓	✓	✓					✓	✓
Festivals and commemorations			✓	✓					✓	✓
Jihad	✓	✓		✓				✓		✓

Topics	AQA AS	AQA A	Eduqas AS	Eduqas A	OCR AS	OCR A	Pearson Edexcel AS	Pearson Edexcel A	WJEC AS	WJEC A
6 Developments and diversity										
Muslim unity during the lifetime of Muhammad					✓	✓				
The early Sunni/Shi'a split			✓	✓	✓	✓		✓	✓	✓
The Rightly Guided Caliphate				✓	✓	✓		✓	✓	✓
Umayyad and Abbasid dynasties								✓		
Interpretations of the Qur'an					✓	✓				
Sufism	✓	✓	✓	✓	✓	✓		✓	✓	✓
7 Science										
The relationship between science and Islam				✓		✓		✓		✓
The origin of the universe				✓		✓				✓
Human origins				✓						
Are Islam and science compatible?				✓		✓				✓
8 Ethics										
The five ethical categories	✓	✓	✓	✓			✓	✓	✓	✓
Sanctity of life	✓	✓	✓	✓						
Crime and punishment			✓	✓	✓			✓		✓	✓
9 Gender and feminism in Islam										
Gender in scripture and early Islam				✓		✓		✓		
Family life				✓		✓		✓		
Secularity and contact with the West				✓		✓		✓		
Feminism and equality				✓		✓		✓		
10 Dialogues										
Qur'anic teachings on the meaning of human existence	✓	✓	✓	✓	✓	✓				
The dialogue between Islam and philosophy				✓	✓	✓				
The Islamic Golden Age			✓	✓	✓	✓				
11 State, society and secularisation										
Madinah as the model state						✓				✓
Pluralism						✓		✓		
Non-Muslims in Muslim societies						✓		✓		
Muslims in non-Muslim societies			✓	✓	✓			✓	✓	✓
Issues facing a multi-faith society						✓		✓		

Assessment overview

For all of the exam boards the skills are the same. AO1 refers to knowledge and understanding and AO2 refers to evaluation and analysis. The question words used will reflect whether you should focus on AO1 or AO2.

Assessment Objectives	Skills	Question words
AO1	Knowledge and understanding	Explain, explore, clarify, examine
AO2	Evaluation and analysis	To what extent, discuss, analyse, assess, evaluate, critically analyse, critically assess

However, the number of marks given for AO1 and AO2 depends on the type of question and whether you are sitting the AS or A-level exam.

Exam board	AS exam	A-level exam
AQA	AO1: 15 marks AO2: 15 marks	AO1: 10 marks AO2: 15 marks
Eduqas	AO1: 25 marks AO2: 25 marks	AO1: 20 marks AO2: 30 marks
OCR	AO1: 15 marks AO2: 15 marks	AO1: 16 marks AO2: 24 marks
Pearson Edexcel	Explore: AO1: 8 marks Assess: AO1: 3 marks, AO2: 9 marks Analyse: AO1: 5 marks, AO2: 15 marks	Explore: AO1: 8 marks Clarify: AO1: 10 marks Assess: AO1: 4 marks, AO2: 8 marks Analyse: AO1: 5 marks, AO2: 15 marks Evaluate: AO1: 5 marks, AO2: 25 marks
WJEC	AO1: 15 marks AO2: 15 marks	AO1: 30 marks AO2: 30 marks

The table below indicates the content covered in each chapter according to exam board, type of exam and Assessment Objectives.

Exam board	Level	AO1	AO2	AO1 and AO2
AQA	AS		Ch 3	
	A	Ch 4, 7, 8	Ch 10	
Eduqas	AS	Ch 8	Ch 5	
	A	Ch 1, 2	Ch 3, 4, 5, 6, 7, 8	Ch 9, 11
OCR	AS			Ch 3, 4, 5
	A	Ch 10	Ch 6, 10	Ch 5, 7, 9
Pearson Edexcel	AS	Ch 1, 2, 5		Ch 4
	A	Ch 9		Ch 11
WJEC	AS	Ch 4		
	A		Ch 3	

A-level Religious Studies: Islam

Exam tips: Assessment Objectives

AO1: Knowledge and understanding

For AO1 you will need to explain. An explanation is *not* a description. For example, think about the difference between describing a table to someone and explaining what a table is. A really good explanation:

+ **includes a wide range of knowledge**. Use specialist language and technical terminology correctly, throughout your answer. It is also a good idea to give examples to show that you know and understand what these technical terms mean
+ **includes a range of religious ideas and beliefs**. Select the right information to answer the question. This means that you should *never* just write everything you know, but instead select the key information needed to address the question
+ **develops key ideas and beliefs to show a depth of understanding**. Give examples and make connections between different concepts. Examples do not need to be long or complex but need to show that you understand the concept. For example, Muslims aim to connect with Allah, which is achieved through Salah. Making connections between concepts shows that you have a deeper understanding of the concepts. For example, risalah links to akhirah because following God's message in this life affects the next life
+ **includes scholarly views and quotes**. This could be quotes from Muslim writers or from the Qur'an, Hadith or Muslim scholars. If you cannot remember quotes word for word, then paraphrase them, giving an idea of what they said. These are also called sources of wisdom and authority.

AO2 Evaluation and analysis

For AO2 you need to discuss, evaluate and analyse. A really good evaluation includes:

+ **arguments for and against**. Why might people agree and disagree with a particular point of view?
+ the **strengths and weaknesses of an idea**. Why might something make sense, be logical or rational? Or why does it not make sense, is not logical or rational?
+ **critical analysis**. For example, explain why there is a weakness or strength rather than just saying what that weakness or strength is. Be critical of criticisms: ask how valid the criticisms are and how much they challenge a set of ideas. Critical analysis:
    + evaluates strengths and weaknesses
    + weighs one piece of information against another
    + makes reasoned judgements
    + shows why something is relevant or suitable
    + identifies whether something is appropriate or suitable
    + weighs up the importance of the component parts
    + evaluates the relative significance of details
    + shows the relevance of links between pieces of information
    + gives the reasons for selecting each option.

Get the most from this book

Everyone has to decide his or her own revision strategy, but it is essential to review your work, learn it and test your understanding. These Revision Notes will help you to do that in a planned way, topic by topic. Use this book as the cornerstone of your revision and don't hesitate to write in it – personalise your notes and check your progress by ticking off each section as you revise.

Tick to track your progress

Use the revision planner on pages 3 and 4 to plan your revision, topic by topic. Tick each box when you have:

+ revised and understood a topic
+ tested yourself
+ practised the exam questions and gone online to check your answers.

You can also keep track of your revision by ticking off each topic heading in the book. You may find it helpful to add your own notes as you work through each topic.

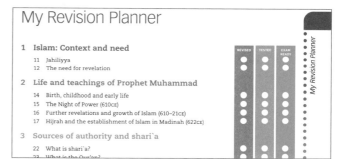

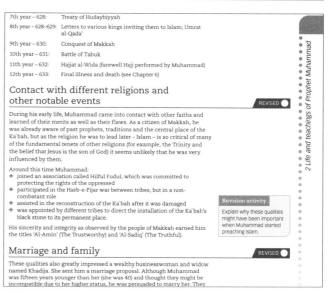

Features to help you succeed

Tips

Expert tips are given throughout the book to help you polish your exam technique in order to maximise your chances in the exam.

Now test yourself

These short, knowledge-based questions provide the first step in testing your learning. Answers are available online.

Definitions and key words

Clear, concise definitions of essential key terms are provided where they first appear.

Key words from the specifications are highlighted in bold throughout the book.

Revision activities

These activities will help you to understand each topic in an interactive way.

Exam practice

Practice exam questions are provided for each topic categorised by the relevant exam board. Use them to consolidate your revision and practise your exam skills.

Summaries

The summaries provide a quick-check bullet list for each topic.

Finally, you can go online to find suggested answers to exam practice at www.hoddereducation.co.uk/myrevisionnotesdownloads

A-level Religious Studies: Islam

Notes

1 Islam: Context and need

Islam is the religion that Muslims believe Allah has chosen for humanity. Muslims believe that all prophets, beginning with Adam, had taught Islam to a limited degree for many centuries (see Chapter 4), but that the faith reached its completion and perfection through Muhammad in seventh-century Arabia. Within his lifetime, Islam had spread throughout the Arabian Peninsula and less than three decades after his death, it had become established in other parts of Asia, North Africa and Europe, thus spanning three continents. This was through military expeditions, trade and migration. It is estimated that there are 1.8 billion Muslims today, making up almost a quarter of the global population and confirming Islam as the world's largest religion after Christianity.

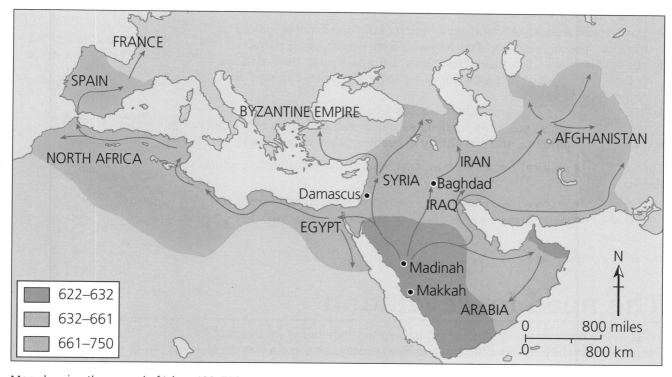

Map showing the spread of Islam 622–750CE

Jahiliyya

Muslims commonly refer to the pre-Islamic period in sixth-century Arabia as Jahiliyya, or 'ignorance'. Around the time of Muhammad, though Arab society had some respectable features, it was less admired in many others.

Arabs were keen businesspeople and commercial carnivals were very popular. Makkah was a successful city of trade. Arabs had high regard for their own honour as well as responsibilities. In a society governed by tribes, chieftains would grant protection to anyone who sought it and visitors were always treated with great hospitality. Arabs took great pride in their culture and language; most literature was preserved and transmitted through oral traditions such as speech and poetry, which was also used as a form of news, entertainment and teaching history. Some poems were hung on the walls of the Ka'bah (centre of worship in Makkah).

> **Jahiliyya** State of ignorance according to Muslims which pre-dated the coming of the Prophet
>
> **Ka'bah** Cube-shaped building in Makkah, which Muslims face towards while praying

A-level Religious Studies: Islam

Arabs were great orators and held regular competitions for the best speeches and poems. They were so advanced in eloquence that they called the rest of the world `ajami (dumb and mute). Poets were among the most influential people in Arabia. Much of the poetry from this period was put in written form later on.

However, there were several problems in Arab society. These included:

+ political instability and lack of social security – there was no unified state or authority as in the modern world, only a tribal system. Social groupings were based on clans loyal to their ancestors
+ nomadic lifestyles – many people lived a nomadic (moving from place to place), herding lifestyle, such as the Bedouin tribes who pastured camels, sheep or goats by using the scanty water resources of the desert, but some also earned their income by raiding other tribes
+ absence of an education system – as in many other societies, no schools existed, resulting in high rates of illiteracy
+ low status of women – unless they were from noble families or were successful in business, women were often treated as inferior to men. Incest and sex outside marriage were common
+ female infanticide – practised by some poor families who wanted boys rather than girls as a way out of poverty
+ slavery, extreme poverty and exploitation of the disadvantaged (for example, poorer) sections of society who were denied equal rights
+ abuse of animals – in some tribes it was customary upon the death of a person to tie his camel close to his grave to be left to die of hunger and thirst
+ violence, cruelty and cannibalism – tribes would go to war over the smallest disputes and would mutilate as well as eat the bodies of the dead
+ alcoholism, gambling and dishonesty in business were widespread.

These were the political, social, economic and moral characteristics to which the Qur'an refers:

> Corruption has flourished on land and sea as a result of people's actions and He (God) will make them taste the consequences of some of their own actions so that they may turn back.

(Qur'an 30: 41, Haleem 2008)

> **Qur'an** Muslim sacred text and most important source of authority in Islam

> **Revision activity**
>
> What features of Jahiliyya come under the following characteristics?
> + Political
> + Social
> + Economic
> + Moral

The need for revelation

Religion in Arabia was very ritualistic. Many Arabs were proud followers of the prophet Ibrahim (Abraham), who had lived in Makkah some 4,000 years ago. However, they did not think it was possible to communicate directly with Allah (God) as Ibrahim had done, due to his status as a prophet. They had not had a monotheistic teacher for a long time, and this led to the gradual rise of polytheism (belief in multiple gods) and the worship of 360 idols who they believed were the only means to reach God. These idols were housed in the Ka`bah, and animal and human sacrifices were offered to them. Pilgrims from all over Arabia would visit to pay homage to these gods and, as there were only a few temples at the time, the Ka`bah assumed a central place in the spiritual life of many Arabs.

> **Polytheism** Belief in multiple gods

This gave Makkah an important status; the city was among the most advanced in Arabia and was part of a region considered sacred due to its proximity to the Ka`bah. The custodianship of the Ka`bah was seen as a great privilege and the housing of the idols brought the city respect as well as revenue.

Many Arabs named their children after these gods, for example, 'Abd Manat' (son of Manat, one of the three supposed 'daughters' of God). Pagan beliefs, which included animism (belief that non-human entities, such as animals and plants have a spiritual essence) and faith in jinns (spirits believed to exist on Earth) were very popular, especially among the Bedouin tribes.

The three main religions at the time were:

+ Judaism – first founded by Abraham (Ibrahim) and later established by Moses (Musa). Both are mentioned in the Old Testament. Jews believe they were God's chosen people to be in a special covenant with Him. Jewish tribes in Arabia had initially migrated from Syria and were influential over the economic life of the region of Hijaz.

+ Christianity – founded by Isa (Jesus) who is the main figure mentioned in the New Testament. Christians believe him to be the Messiah and the son of God. In Arabia, the region of Najran was the main centre of Christianity. It is said that statues of Isa and his mother Maryam (Mary) were also housed in the Ka`bah.

+ Zoroastrianism – founded by the Iranian prophet Zoroaster. It involved the worship of the god Ahura Mazda who required the good deeds of his followers to help in his cosmic struggle against the evil spirit Ahriman.

These religions had moved away from their monotheistic origins and developed practices that were regarded as idolatrous, apparently influenced by Arab culture at the time. Among these traditions were People of the Book devoted to the remembrance of one God (Qur'an 3: 113–15) and strict monotheists (believers in one God) known as 'Hanifs', though these were few in number.

The existing religions did not do a great deal to address the widespread problems in Arabia. Muslims believed there was a need for a new revelation that would meet the spiritual, moral, intellectual and social needs of all people – not just particular communities, as with Christianity whose message was confined to the lost sheep of Israel (Matthew 10: 5–6) – and that this was fulfilled with the appearance of Muhammad.

> *Remember that God revives the earth after it dies.*

(Qur'an 57: 17, Haleem 2008)

> **Animism** Belief that spirits exist in animate and inanimate objects
>
> **Jinns** Spirits or hidden beings
>
> **Monotheists** Believers in one God

Now test yourself TESTED ◯

1 List three reasons why Muslims believe seventh-century Arabia was in need of reform.

Chapter summary

+ The Jahaliyya is the period of ignorance Muslims believe Arabia was in prior to Islam.
+ Arab society mostly suffered from many problems including tribal feuds, the absence of an education system, and the denial of equal rights to many sections of society, including women and slaves.
+ The conditions at the time necessitated in a new faith that would meet the spiritual, moral, intellectual and social needs of all people.

Exam practice

In your exam, you may be asked about pre-Islamic Arabia. Some example questions include:

Explain why Muslims believe there was a need for revelation at the time of Muhammad. [Eduqas, AO1, 20 marks]

Explore the status of Makkah at the time of Muhammad. [Pearson Edexcel, AO1, 8 marks]

2 Life and teachings of Prophet Muhammad

Birth, childhood and early life

Most accounts trace Muhammad's birth to Makkah in either 570 or 571CE. The name Muhammad means 'most praiseworthy' and was told to his mother Aminah in a dream. His family belonged to the Quraysh (a ruling Arab tribe).

Muslims believe that when Muhammad was four years old, an angel was seen to cut open Muhammad's chest and clean his heart. This was similar to what was to happen at other times in his life including during the Mi`raj experience, although these events have been interpreted by some to be visions and symbolic of his body being filled with light and wisdom.

By the time of his birth, it is believed Muhammad's father Abdullah had died. Muhammad was orphaned by the age of six when his mother died, after which he was raised by his grandfather. His grandfather died two years later. Muhammad was then brought up by his uncle Abu Talib. He spent his youth tending to cattle and goats but started to accompany and assist Abu Talib on trading trips between Arabia and Syria, where the Quraysh had their biggest business ties. He also went to Yemen and Bahrain. For some time, Muhammad worked as a camel driver and then managed caravans on behalf of merchants. He developed a reputation as an honest and successful trader. He was employed by Khadija, a wealthy businesswoman.

Muhammad's life – timeline

REVISED ●

The Makkan years

1st year – 610:	Night of Power experience and beginning of preaching
6th year – 615:	First Muslim migration to Abyssinia; Mi'raj (ascension) experience
10th year – 619:	Death of wife Khadija and uncle Abu Talib during social boycott of Muslims
11th year – 620:	Isra' (night journey)
12th year – 621:	Meeting with people of Yathrib and first pledge at 'Aqabah

The Madinan years

1st year – 622:	Hijrah and arrival at Madinah; second pledge at 'Aqabah; built Quba Mosque and Prophet's Mosque; first call to prayer; establishment of fraternity between Ansar (Muslims of Madinah) and Muhajirun (Muslim migrants from Makkah); signed treaty with Jews of the area
2nd year – 623:	Marriage to Aishah (see Chapter 9)
3rd year – 624:	Change of the qiblah (prayer direction) from Jerusalem to Makkah; first Id-ul-Fitr (see Chapter 5); Battle of Badr (see Chapter 5)
4th year – 625:	Battle of Uhud
5th year – 626:	Expulsion of Banu Nadir from Madinah (see Chapter 11)
6th year – 627:	Battle of the Ditch and punishment of Banu Qurayzah (see Chapter 11)

Suggested answer guidance to exam practice at **www.hoddereducation.co.uk/myrevisionnotesdownloads**

7th year – 628:	Treaty of Hudaybiyyah
8th year – 628–629:	Letters to various kings inviting them to Islam; Umrat al-Qada'
9th year – 630:	Conquest of Makkah
10th year – 631:	Battle of Tabuk
11th year – 632:	Hajjat al-Wida (farewell Hajj performed by Muhammad)
12th year – 633:	Final illness and death (see Chapter 6)

Contact with different religions and other notable events

REVISED

During his early life, Muhammad came into contact with other faiths and learned of their merits as well as their flaws. As a citizen of Makkah, he was already aware of past prophets, traditions and the central place of the Ka`bah, but as the religion he was to lead later – Islam – is so critical of many of the fundamental tenets of other religions (for example, the Trinity and the belief that Jesus is the son of God) it seems unlikely that he was very influenced by them.

Around this time Muhammad:
+ joined an association called Hilful Fudul, which was committed to protecting the rights of the oppressed
+ participated in the Harb-e-Fijar war between tribes, but in a non-combatant role
+ assisted in the reconstruction of the Ka`bah after it was damaged
+ was appointed by different tribes to direct the installation of the Ka`bah's black stone to its permanent place.

His sincerity and integrity as observed by the people of Makkah earned him the titles 'Al-Amin' (The Trustworthy) and 'Al-Sadiq' (The Truthful).

> **Revision activity**
>
> Explain why these qualities might have been important when Muhammad started preaching Islam.

Marriage and family

REVISED

These qualities also greatly impressed his employer Khadija. Having been widowed, she sent him a marriage proposal. Although Muhammad was fifteen years younger than her (she was 40) and thought they might be incompatible due to her higher status, he was persuaded to marry her. They had a loving and happy marriage and although polygamy was common at the time, Muhammad did not marry again until her death 25 years later. Through their marriage Muhammad became rich but he used his wealth to free slaves and help the poor. Together they had six children – four daughters and two sons – although the boys all died in infancy.

> **Now test yourself**
>
> TESTED
>
> 1 What qualities made Muhammad popular with people?
> 2 Who was Khadija? Limit your answer to 50 words.
> 3 Give two examples of Muhammad's care and concern for society's most disadvantaged.

The Night of Power (610CE)

Muhammad was quiet and reflective and often visited a nearby cave, Hira, to spend time in solitude and the remembrance of one God, away from the worship of idols in and around the Ka`bah. He was dissatisfied with life in Makkah as it was full of corruption and immorality and used this time to

15

search for solutions through prayer and to seek a deeper connection with Allah.

Did He not find you an orphan and shelter you?

(Qur'an 93: 6, Haleem 2008)

During one of these retreats in Ramadan (the ninth month in the Islamic year), Muhammad, aged 40, had a powerful religious experience. He received a visit by the angel Jibril (Gabriel) who instructed 'Iqra!', meaning 'Proclaim!' or 'Read!', three times. Muhammad, who was illiterate, was unsure what was being said. Jibril continued 'Read! In the name of your Lord who created: He created man from a clinging form. Read! Your Lord is the Most Bountiful One who taught by [means of] the pen, who taught man what he did not know.' (Qur'an 96: 1–5). The message meant that Muhammad was being told to convey the message of God's oneness to the people. He responded hesitantly, saying that he could not. The experience overwhelmed Muhammad and he wanted to run home, but Jibril informed him that he had been chosen as a prophet. When he got home Muhammad was shivering and had to be comforted by Khadjia who wrapped him in a blanket. After hearing what happened and observing his confusion, she reassured him that he was not possessed by anything satanic; instead, he had been appointed by Allah for a special purpose.

God is witness, He has not sent you this Word that you should fail and prove unworthy, that He should then give you up. How can God do such a thing, while you are kind and considerate to your relations, help the poor and the forlorn and bear their burdens? You are restoring the virtues which had disappeared from our country. You treat guests with honour and help those who are in distress. Can you be subjected by God to any trial?

(Bukhari)

Khadija took Muhammad to her Christian relative, Waraqah bin Nawfal, who after hearing what had happened, said that it appeared that Muhammad had been chosen as a prophet. This event is known as the Night of Power (Laylat al-Qadr) and proved to be a turning point, not just for Muhammad but for Makkah and Islam as well.

> **Night of Power (Laylat al-Qadr)** The night the Prophet received his first Qur'anic revelation

We sent it down on the Night of Glory. What will explain to you what the Night of Glory is? The Night of Glory is better than a thousand months; on that night the angels and the Spirit descend again and again with their Lord's permission on every task; Peace it is until the rising of the dawn.

(Qur'an 97: 1–5, Haleem 2008)

Now test yourself	TESTED ○

4 Why might this experience have been called the Night of Power?
5 How might Khadija's words have comforted Muhammad?

Further revelations and growth of Islam (610–21CE)

After his initial anxieties, Muhammad accepted that he had been chosen as a prophet and messenger. More revelations followed and the messages he received addressed many of the problems he perceived in his society, such as idolatry, inequality and injustice. For the first three years, Muhammad shared these teachings secretively. Once he had gained some followers, he began to teach openly (Qur'an 15: 94). He taught people strict monotheism, challenged the worship of idols, emphasised a strong moral code, promoted service to all of creation and taught that there was hope for eternal life after death.

> Those they invoke beside God create nothing; they are themselves created. They are dead, not living. They do not know when they will be raised up. Your God is the One God.

(Qur'an 16: 20–22, Haleem 2008)

Initially the weaker members of society, such as the poor, accepted him, but soon influential figures joined the new religion too. Those who accepted him became known as Muslims. This did not sit well with the Makkan leaders who were very defensive of their way of life. Reasons for their rejection of Muhammad included:

+ the worship of idols was entrenched in their culture and also brought money
+ they were proud of maintaining the traditions of their ancestors
+ they were contented with the social status quo of masters owning slaves and living luxuriously
+ Muhammad was not a chieftain or man of high status, so he was not worthy of attention.

Initially they merely mocked Muhammad, but as they began to worry about his increasing popularity, they offered him authority, money, beautiful women, and more, on the condition he stopped preaching. Muhammad declined, insisting that his message was from Allah, and continued undeterred. The leaders were insulted by this rejection and believed that the new faith Islam posed a threat to their position and the reputation of the city. They began a campaign of persecution.

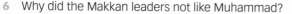

Now test yourself   TESTED ◯

6   Why did the Makkan leaders not like Muhammad?
7   Why did Muhammad turn down their offers?

The first targets were the poorer Muslims who were subjected to verbal as well as physical abuse and torture, and many were murdered. A three-year social boycott was enforced during which Muslim properties were attacked and businesses were forbidden to sell their goods to Muslims. It was during this period of oppression that both Khadija and Abu Talib died.

Far from arresting the growth of Islam, cruelty towards Muslims created more sympathy and curiosity about the new faith, and more people converted. This included people from other parts of Arabia, particularly Yathrib – around 250 miles from Makkah – who visited Muhammad at 'Aqabah to pledge allegiance to him.

These people were mainly representatives of tribes who were at war and desperately sought mediation. They also believed Muhammad was the Musa-like prophet foretold in the Tawrat (Torah).

> We shall believe in one God, shall not associate partners with God, shall not steal, shall not commit adultery or fornication, shall abstain from murder, shall not defame anyone, and shall obey you in everything good.

(First Pledge at 'Aqabah)

Within the first thirteen years of his preaching, the number of Muslims in Makkah was relatively low (approximately 100) but had grown to around 800 in Yathrib.

Revision activity

What parts of this pledge were a challenge to the life and customs in Arabia?

A-level Religious Studies: Islam

Hijrah and the establishment of Islam in Madinah (622CE)

The Makkan leaders intensified their efforts to end Islam and it became clear that it was unsafe for Muslims to stay in Makkah. Throughout this period of persecution, Muslims did not retaliate and maintained a policy of non-violence. The Prophet Muhammad himself continued to pray earnestly for his enemies to change their attitude (Qur'an 18: 6).

Muhammad and the first Muslims were commanded by Allah to leave the city in secret and settle elsewhere. Some had already been instructed to migrate to Abyssinia, but the majority of Muslims, including Muhammad, decided upon Yathrib. Muhammad was invited to a second meeting at 'Aqabah, by its leaders, and was promised protection and their loyalty. Muslims left the city a few at a time. Muhammad was one of the last Muslims to leave Makkah, as he wanted to put the safety of others first. This historic journey is known as the hijrah (migration) and marks the start of the Islamic calendar.

> Remember [Prophet] when the disbelievers plotted to take you captive, kill, or expel you. They schemed and so did God: He is the best of schemers.

(Qur'an 8: 30, Haleem 2008)

Muhammad was accompanied by his friend Abu Bakr. The journey took eight days. There were efforts to track and capture or kill them, but none of these succeeded. When Muhammad arrived at Yathrib, its people welcomed him with open arms and unanimously agreed to appoint him as the leader of the city. Yathrib was renamed Madinat al-Nabi, literally 'City of the Prophet', or simply Madinah ('City'). Three key events marked this new chapter in Islam:

1 The first central mosque – Al-Masjid al-Nabawi (Prophet's Mosque) – was built, which would become the religious, social, political and legal centre of Islam.
2 Fraternity was established between the Muhajirun or migrants (Muslims from Makkah) and Ansar or helpers (Muslims of Madinah) – each helper would take in a migrant and treat them like a member of their own family.
3 The Constitution of Madinah was drawn up by Muhammad, and effectively established a unified sovereign state, based on the principle of justice as instructed by the Qur'an (Qur'an 16: 91). The new government defined the rights and responsibilities of all citizens and also stated that Madinah was a multi-faith city, made up mainly of Muslim, Jewish and pagan people, in which freedom of belief thrived.

Although every community in the city was free in terms of its religious and internal affairs, they were regulated by a common law and central government, headed by Muhammad.

The Constitution stated:
+ Muslims and Jews would live together with sympathy and sincerity and would not oppress or wrong each other
+ all people would enjoy religious freedom
+ the lives and wealth of all citizens would be honoured and safeguarded, except if someone was guilty of oppression or criminality
+ all disputes and conflicts would be presented to Muhammad for his judgement, with all verdicts in accordance with Divine Command in the Qur'an and Tawrat
+ nobody would set out for war without Muhammad's permission
+ if another nation waged war against the Jews or Muslims, each would defend the other
+ if Madinah was attacked, everyone would defend it collectively

Hijrah The journey from Makkah to Madinah by the Prophet and other Muslims in the year 622CE. The Muslim calendar is called the hijri calendar because it begins from this date

Constitution of Madinah An agreement drawn up by the Prophet for the people of Madinah

Revision activity

Write a brief explanation of how these three events helped the growth of Islam in Madinah.

Suggested answer guidance to exam practice at **www.hoddereducation.co.uk/myrevisionnotesdownloads**

- the Jews would not provide any aid or protection to the Quraysh of Makkah or their allies
- every community would bear their own expenses
- no tyrant, criminal or wrongdoer would be protected from punishment or retribution.

The migration was significant for Muhammad and the Muslims. Whereas in Makkah the Prophet's message enjoyed limited success due to the city's oppressive rulers, Madinah offered a safe harbour and ideal context for Islamic theocracy to flourish, despite being a minority faith, and play a role in the secular as well as religious life of the city.

The revelations no longer covered only personal spiritual matters but started to address the public sphere. This reinforced the belief that Islam had become a complete way of life.

Muhammad as leader

In addition to his religious status as a prophet, Muhammad proved himself to be a very able politician, statesman and moral guide. With the signing of the constitution, he was able to unite the conflicting tribes of the city. The theocracy strengthened and his reputation spread rapidly. Muslims believe his benevolent personality and democratic style of leadership made him both popular and successful.

> Out of mercy from God, you [Prophet] were gentle in your dealings with them – had you been harsh, or hard-hearted, they would have dispersed and left you – so pardon them and ask forgiveness for them. Consult with them about matters, then, when you have decided on a course of action, put your trust in God; God loves those who put their trust in Him.

(Qur'an 3: 159, Haleem 2008)

For the first few months, Muslims lived in peace and security, but the leaders in Makkah, not content with the migration, had amassed an army to attack Madinah and to try to end Islam once and for all. Muhammad now assumed a military role to lead a Muslim army to fight in self-defence. Even though the Muslims were outnumbered, they defeated their enemies, first at Badr and then after a setback at Uhud (in which Muhammad himself was wounded), they succeeded in subsequent wars. The last battle led by Muhammad was the Battle of Tabuk, when he was about 60 years of age.

In 629, Muhammad and 1,500 Muslims proceeded towards Makkah to perform umrah (lesser pilgrimage), based on a pilgrimage that Muhammad had made in a dream. The Makkan leaders prevented their entry but offered a ten-year peace agreement known as the Treaty of Hudaybiya. This gave permission for Muslims to perform the pilgrimage the following year, which took place as agreed and is known as the Umrat al-Qada'. It was during this period that Muhammad wrote letters to the rulers of neighbouring countries informing them of his mission and inviting them to Islam.

Umrah Lesser pilgrimage to Makkah

Return to Makkah

The pact was broken when Makkans attacked allies of Muhammad. With the Makkan leaders showing no regard for the treaty and more and more people converting to Islam, Muhammad marched to Makkah with 10,000 Muslims. It was a bloodless coup with Muhammad granting a general pardon to the people who had persecuted Muslims – an act of forgiveness that some non-Muslim historians consider unparalleled. All idols in the Ka`bah were destroyed to restore it as a house for the worship of one God.

Even in this moment of triumph, Muhammad did not forget his first wife Khadija, who had been his rock throughout their marriage, as well as his first believer. Despite numerous offers of hospitality from his followers, he chose to spend time in a tent pitched next to Khadija's grave in Hajun cemetery, which is also known by the name of Jannat al-Mu'allah.

Just before his death, in his Last Sermon delivered on the occasion of Hajj, Muhammad said:

> All mankind is from Adam and Eve. An Arab has no superiority over a non-Arab nor a non-Arab has any superiority over an Arab; also a white has no superiority over black nor a black has any superiority over white except by piety and good action.

(The Last Sermon)

Muhammad died in 632CE. By this time almost the entire population of Makkah had become Muslim. Within two years, Islamic rule had spread over the entire Arabian Peninsula and Islam was the dominant religion. Muhammad's successes and achievements as a prophet, moral guide, politician and military commander earned him respect as an outstanding leader.

> Philosopher, Orator, Apostle, Legislator, Conqueror of Ideas, Restorer of Rational beliefs …. The founder of twenty terrestrial empires and of one spiritual empire – that is Muhammad. As regards all standards by which human greatness may be measured, we may well ask, is there any man greater than he?

(Alphonse de Lamartine, French author and statesman, 1854)

Karen Armstrong said that 'Muhammad was frequently in deadly peril and his survival was a near miracle. But he did succeed.'

Now test yourself TESTED ◯

8 Give at least one example of Muhammad's:
   + religious leadership
   + moral leadership
   + political leadership
   + military leadership.

Chapter summary

+ Muhammad demonstrated many great qualities prior to prophethood, including honesty and faithfulness.
+ The Night of Power experience and his appointment as a messenger signalled a turning point for Muhammad and also life in Makkah and beyond.
+ His teachings led to persecution by the leaders of Makkah, causing Muslims to migrate to Madinah where Muhammad headed a new state.
+ A number of battles were fought between Muslims and the non-believers and the Prophet and his followers were able to return victoriously to Makkah, where the Ka'bah was restored as a house for the worship of one God.

Exam practice

For a question which focuses just on AO1 you need to demonstrate the following:

+ A wide range of knowledge: this can be shown by using specialist language and technical terminology correctly throughout your answer. Giving examples to show that you know and understand what these technical terms mean is also good.
+ Knowledge and understanding of a range of religious ideas and beliefs: you can show this by selecting the right information to answer the question. This means that you should never just write everything you know, but instead select the key information needed to address the question.
+ Develop key religious ideas and beliefs to show a depth of understanding of key religious ideas and beliefs: you can do this by giving examples and making connections between different concepts. Examples do not need to be long or complex but need to show that you understand the concept. For example, hijrah refers to when persecuted Muslims left Makkah for a safer life elsewhere. In your answer you should refer to the circumstances that led to the hijrah, any important events during it and the impact it had on Muhammad and the early Muslim community. For example, you could discuss the impact of the move from Makkah to Madinah on Muhammad's role and the growth of Islam.

A higher-level answer should also, where appropriate:

+ demonstrate thorough, accurate and relevant knowledge and understanding
+ be extensive and relevant, and answer the specific demands of the question
+ have extensive depth and/or breadth, and make excellent use of evidence and examples
+ make thorough and accurate reference to the Qur'an and other sources of wisdom
+ make insightful connections between the various approaches studied
+ include an extensive range of views of scholars/schools of thought used accurately and effectively
+ make thorough and accurate use of specialist language and vocabulary in context.

Here are a couple of examples of AO1 questions:

Explain the significance of the hijrah. [Eduqas, AO1, 20]

+ In your answer you should refer to the circumstances that led to the hijrah, any important events during it and the impact it had on Muhammad and the early Muslim community. For example, you could discuss the impact of the move from Makkah to Madinah on Muhammad's role and the growth of Islam.

Explore the main features of the accounts of Muhammad's Night of Power.
[Pearson Edexcel, AO1, 8]

+ In your answer you should refer to Muhammad's reasons for retreating to Cave Hira and include key information about what happened during the first Qur'anic revelation (angel Jibril's visit).

What is shari`a?

Shari`a is a code for living based on the concept of Islam as a complete way of life. It covers all aspects of day-to-day living, public and private, from the spiritual (prayer, fasting, pilgrimage) to the secular (politics, banking, business). Shari`a sets out the behaviour and actions expected of Muslims at all levels – personal, social, national and global, so is often called shari`a law. It means 'the way' or 'the path to a water source'.

> *Guide us to the straight path: the path of those You have blessed.*

(Qur'an 1: 6–7, Haleem 2008)

Shari`a is underpinned by two key obligations:
+ Huquq Allah (serving and fulfilling the rights of God)
+ Huquq al-`Ibad (serving and fulfilling the rights of his creation).

Seyyed Hossein Nasr says that 'all human activity must be carried out in accordance with the Will as embodied in the Divine Law [shari`a]' and that 'Human action must be pleasing and acceptable in God's eyes.'

> **Shari`a** 'The way to water', referring to the Islamic legal system

The sources of shari`a

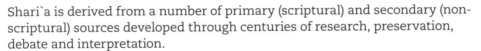 REVISED

Shari`a is derived from a number of primary (scriptural) and secondary (non-scriptural) sources developed through centuries of research, preservation, debate and interpretation.

> *You who believe, obey God and the Messenger, and those in authority among you. If you are in dispute over any matter, refer it to God and the Messenger, if you truly believe in God and the Last Day: that is better and fairer in the end.*

(Qur'an 4: 59, Haleem 2008)

The sources as accepted by the majority of Muslims are usually found in the following order:

Scriptural
1 Qur'an – believed to be the revealed word of Allah
2 Sunnah – the actions of the Prophet Muhammad
3 Hadith – the sayings of the Prophet Muhammad (also referred to as 'report')
4 Sira – biographies of the life of the Prophet Muhammad

Non-scriptural
5 Ijma' – consensus of the community
6 Qiyas – analogical reasoning
7 Ijtihad – interpretative effort or intellectual struggle
8 Urf – local traditions and customs in the time of the Prophet Muhammad

These are viewed as a hierarchy of sources; if clear guidance is provided in any of the scriptural sources, there is no need to consult non-scriptural ones.

> **Sunnah** Actions of the Prophet
>
> **Hadith** Sayings of the Prophet Muhammad
>
> **Sira** An account of the Prophet's life
>
> **Ijma'** Agreement by consensus of scholars or the community
>
> **Qiyas** Analogical reasoning
>
> **Ijtihad** Interpretative effort or intellectual struggle
>
> **Urf** Local traditions and customs in the time of the Prophet Muhammad

Now test yourself TESTED

1 Explain the relevance of Qur'an 1: 6–7 in relation to shari'a.
2 Which of the scriptural and non-scriptural sources may be referred to in Qur'an 4: 59?

Different views of shari`a

There are different views about shari`a and where and when it should apply. Some say it is purely to guide a Muslim in their personal faith; others argue that it also covers matters relating to society. Many see shari`a as a code for civic, religious and moral life.

+ Shari`a as **civil law** – laws relating to family life and society, including criminal cases. Shari`a courts are set up to help resolve disputes regarding personal matters.
+ Shari`a as **religious law** – Islam teaches the importance of good deeds, and there are five categories of action devised by scholars (see Chapter 8). In some countries, this influences punishments for certain offences, for example, blasphemy.
+ Shari`a as a **moral guide** – at a personal level (for example, making individual choices about how to follow Islam) and a societal level (enforcing a moral code).

There are also disagreements about whether shari`a should be described as law.

> **Fiqh** 'deep understanding' or 'intelligence', later simply known as Muslim jurisprudence or law

For shari`a being described as law:	Against shari`a being described as law:
+ The great lengths taken by classical scholars to compose a comprehensive system for **fiqh** means shari`a should be regarded as a legal code + Shari`a courts exist to ensure Islamic laws are being followed + Some give shari`a ultimate status and support the implementation of shari`a law wherever there are Muslims	+ Is it relevant when secular laws, such as the Universal Declaration of Human Rights, grant religious freedom? + Faith is a personal matter – the Qur'an declares 'There is no compulsion in religion' (Qur'an 2: 256) – so everyone is accountable for themselves + No Muslim country claims to follow shari`a fully. Most countries have their own laws organised through state systems. Some governments consult scholars and muftis (experts in Islamic law) but do not have to accept their advice

Where the Qur'an, Sunnah and Hadith do not give a clear instruction, human interpretation may be necessary. There is debate as to whether this has been successful.

+ Meticulous care was taken by the earlier Muslims to preserve and interpret the sources. They took this role seriously and made great sacrifices.
+ When compiling Hadiths, the criteria was set by people, not Allah or Muhammad.
+ The Qur'an already indicated that Muslims would have disagreements and that there was a solution to this – 'If you are in dispute over any matter, refer it to God and the Messenger' (Qur'an 4: 59).
+ People look for and value experts in various fields – why not in shari`a matters too?
+ Attempts by humans to understand and implement Allah's will have been flawed and led to chaos in the Muslim world due to conflicting opinions from different scholars (Abou El Fadl).

Now test yourself
TESTED

3 Which of the above points support human interpretation and which oppose it? Explain your selection.

> **Revision activity**
>
> Start a mind-map covering each of the sources of shari`a. Build on this as you go through the topic.

What is the Qur'an?

The Qur'an is the main holy book and primary source of guidance in Islam. It is written in Arabic. The Qur'an consists of hundreds of commandments relating mainly to moral and social behaviour, and worship.

+ The Qur'an is divided into 30 parts (ajza) and 114 Surahs (chapters), each consisting of individual ayaat (verses).

23

- The Surahs vary in length. Surah Al-Kawthar (Chapter 108) is the shortest, with only four verses. The longest is Surah Al-Baqarah (Chapter 2) comprising 287 verses.
- With the inclusion of tasmiyya (invoking the name of Allah), there are 6,348 verses in the Qur'an.
- The Makkan revelations are shorter and mainly cover core beliefs such as the oneness of God, while Madinan revelations are longer and focus on more practical matters, such as how to live in accordance with Islamic principles.

Authority of the Qur'an

REVISED

Muslims believe that the Qur'an is Allah's direct revelation to the Prophet Muhammad through the angel Jibril, which was revealed gradually over the last 23 years of his life.

For Muslims, the Qur'an is the highest source of wisdom and authority, free from error and unchangeable (Qur'an 11: 1), the basis of the shari`a and a sign of Allah's omnipotence (power).

> This is the Scripture in which there is no doubt, containing guidance for those who are mindful of God.

(Qur'an 2: 2, Haleem 2008)

> We built the sky with Our power and made it vast.

(Qur'an 51: 47, Haleem 2008)

The Qur'an is described as 'a blessed scripture' (Qur'an 6: 155) and 'a mercy' (Qur'an 29: 51). Muslims believe that it is Allah's final and perfect revelation to humanity and the only scripture meant for all times, all people and all places (unlike previous holy texts – see Chapter 4). To Muslims, Muhammad is a universal messenger who was sent by Allah with a complete message that would have eternal relevance.

Message of the Qur'an

REVISED

For Muslims, the Qur'an offers comprehensive information and guidance on all matters, from the creation of the universe and of human beings, to the right way to worship and how to treat others. This is one of the reasons that Muslims known as Qur'anists use only the Qur'an and do not depend on any other source.

Most of the Qur'an is about the nature and actions of Allah and how people should act in order to have a relationship with Him.

Two of the most notable chapters are the first and second chapters, Surah Al-Fatiha and Surah Al-Baqarah.

Surah Al-Fatiha (Qur'an 1)

- Means 'The Opening' and has seven verses. Some consider it to be similar to the Lord's Prayer in Christianity.
- It was revealed in Makkah and is the most frequently recited Surah in the Salah (see Chapter 5).
- The chapter teaches about God's principal attributes and includes a prayer for guidance as well as protection against evil.
- The Prophet Muhammad referred to this chapter as 'the Great Qur'an' (Hadith – Musnad) as it is a summary of the whole Qur'an.

Surah Al-Baqarah (Qur'an 2)

+ Means 'The Cow' and is the longest chapter in the Qur'an and summarises its teachings.
+ It began to be revealed in the first year of the hijrah in Madinah and was completed only a short time before Muhammad's death.
+ It contains what Muhammad called the 'loftiest verse of the Qur'an', known as ayat al-kursi (Throne Verse).
+ The title of the chapter refers to the time of Musa when his followers began to worship the golden calf, against his wishes. This is interpreted as a warning to Muslims not to make the same error of being disobedient, and to believe in Allah and submit to his will.
+ It also records a prayer of the prophet Ibrahim asking Allah to raise a prophet among the Makkans in the future who should recite God's signs and guide them along a spiritual path that would transform them into a great nation. Muslims believe this prayer was fulfilled with the appearance of Muhammad.
+ The chapter also covers themes such as:
  + the afterlife
  + divine revelations and prophethood
  + injunctions about prayer, fasting and pilgrimage
  + marriage, divorce, inheritance, the care of orphans and widows
  + preparedness for martyrdom
  + prohibition of charging interest on loans.
+ It ends with a comprehensive prayer for believers to be able to discharge their great responsibilities.

The revelation and compilation of the Qur'an

Revelation

REVISED

Muslims believe that the text of the Qur'an was revealed to Muhammad by the angel Jibril piece by piece over a period of 23 years, starting in the cave Hira (see Chapter 2). It is said that each revelation was a powerful experience which overwhelmed Muhammad. Muslims believe that this shows that the Qur'an was not the product of his imagination, but the words of Allah (Qur'an 10: 37–8, 15: 9).

Compilation

REVISED

Muhammad dictated the revelations to many scribes (over 40), who recorded them very carefully, and great efforts were made to preserve them word for word. Because oral tradition was so important in Arabic culture, many Arabs were able to memorise long passages. Many of the first Muslims were able to commit the entire text of the Qur'an to memory.

The Qur'an does not contain the revelations in the order they were received; Jibril told Muhammad where each verse was to appear. Jibril visited the Prophet Muhammad every year during Ramadan to rehearse the revelations, and in the last year of Muhammad's life, the angel did this twice. It was only after his death that all the recorded pieces of the Qur'an were compiled into a book, in the order Muhammad had instructed.

The compilation was prioritised by the first three 'Rightly Guided Caliphs'. The third Caliph, Uthman, authorised one standardised version of the Qur'an to be printed and distributed throughout the ummah (worldwide body of Muslims). This copy became known as the Uthmanic codex and is also called the al-Mushaf al-Uthmani.

Caliph (Khalifah) successor of the Prophet (Sunni)

Ummah Originally, the citizens of Madinah under the Prophet's authority, later evolved to mean the worldwide Muslim community

Preservation

REVISED

Muslims believe that fourteen centuries after its revelation, the entire text of the Qur'an remains unchanged. This is a fulfilment of a promise made by Allah, that it would not be distorted by humans:

> *We have sent down the Qur'an Ourself, and We Ourself will guard it.*

(Qur'an 15: 9, Haleem 2008)

In 2015, researchers at the University of Birmingham discovered one of the earliest known Qur'anic manuscripts from around the time of Muhammad. The text they found, Surahs 18 to 20, is the same as the words in the Qur'an read by Muslims today.

The original Qur'anic text has stayed intact because of:
+ Uthman's adoption of a single version of the Qur'an across the Muslim world
+ the fact that Sunni and Shi'a Muslims accept and read the same version today
+ the tradition of Hifz (committing the entire Qur'an to memory) in Muslim communities around the world
+ the obligatory recitation of the Qur'an in Salah (five daily prayers) and during tarawih (additional night prayers) during Ramadan
+ the confirmation of reformers (mujaddids) and other saintly figures throughout Muslim history.

The treatment of the Qur'an

Muslims treat the Qur'an with the utmost respect. Many perform wudu (ablution) before touching the Qur'an. The Qur'an is:
+ recited melodiously (Qur'an 73: 4)
+ kissed by many after its recitation
+ covered in a cloth to keep it clean
+ kept as high as possible, such as on the top shelf of a bookcase, as a symbol of its authority
+ never allowed to touch the floor.

> *The best among you is the one who learns the Qur'an and teaches it.*

(Hadith – Bukhari)

Translation and commentary

REVISED

Today the Qur'an has been translated into several languages, though this did not start until the eighteenth century. When the Muslim reformer Shah Wali Ullah Dehlawi translated the Qur'an into Persian in 1738, he faced fierce opposition from orthodox scholars as they considered translation to be impossible and forbidden.

Despite the popularity of certain translations, all Muslims agree that no translation can ever do justice to the Qur'anic text and message, and that they merely represent interpretations and offer only one possible meaning of the original. This is because of the rich breadth of meanings of Arabic words. Muslims are encouraged to learn Arabic and many Islamic publishers print the original Arabic alongside any translation.

Some editions of the Qur'an include a detailed commentary (tafsir) by scholars known as mufassireen who are considered qualified to explain the text. Commentaries aim to compensate, though never fully, for the limitations of a translation.

Now test yourself

TESTED

4 Give three reasons why the Qur'an is the highest authority for Muslims.

5 Why are Muslims convinced of the divine nature of the Qur'an and how is this expressed in daily practice?

Suggested answer guidance to exam practice at **www.hoddereducation.co.uk/myrevisionnotesdownloads**

What are the Sunnah and Hadith?

In addition to the Qur'an, Muhammad's actions and sayings have been recorded so that Muslims can use his character and teachings as a basis for living. This is why belief in both tawhid and Muhammad's prophethood, as captured in the Shahadah (see Chapter 5), is essential for Muslims.

+ The **Sunnah** describe the way Muhammad lived, what he did and did not do.
+ The **Hadith** mainly capture his words.

Some Muslims consider the Sunnah and Hadith to be separate and others classify Hadith as part of the Sunnah.

Like the Qur'an, the Sunnah and Hadith provide detailed guidance on a wide range of matters from the spiritual to the social and the personal to the political. Muhammad's private and public conduct, how he worshipped, treated his followers and enemies and the words he spoke, are found mainly in the Sunnah and Hadith.

Consolidation and compilation

 REVISED

The Sunnah were based on the way that Muhammad spoke, acted, dressed and prayed. They were learned through direct observation of him during his lifetime and became established as they were imitated and adopted by successive generations of Muslims.

The Hadith took longer to become established. The Hadith are narrated by the sahabah (companions) of Muhammad, before being passed down to the next generation of Muslims known as Tabi'in (those who observed the sahabah), and from them to the following generation. These generations are known by the term 'salaf' and are highly honoured by Muslims for preserving the Prophet's guidance.

The compilation of Hadith started about 100 years after the hijrah and continued up to about 300 years after the hijrah. However, before they could be published, important checks needed to be made by Muhaddithun (Hadith experts) to distinguish genuine accounts from unreliable and forged ones. The classification of Hadiths was very thorough and was based on establishing the chain of narrators (isnad) of each Hadith, back to the Prophet Muhammad or his companions (tawatur).

Hadiths would generally be accepted if the isnad and tawatur were sound and where there were multiple reporters of the same event. However, they would be questioned if they:
+ opposed or contradicted the teachings of the Qur'an, Sunnah and collective action of the sahabah
+ opposed or contradicted a proven incident
+ were against common sense.

Hadiths were categorised from sahih (authentic) to dhaif (weak). Most Hadiths which conflict with the Qur'an were rejected, but there could be exceptions, if they came from a trusted source. This is because of the belief that these Hadiths needed to be interpreted differently and understood in their context. For example, the Qur'an declares freedom of belief (Qur'an 2: 285) while some Hadiths state that apostates (those who left Islam) should be put to death. One explanation for this is that Muhammad sometimes followed the Jewish laws in the Tawrat before they were replaced by guidance from new revelations.

Similarly, dhaif Hadiths would no longer be considered weak if they contained information which later turned out to be true.

Sahabah Muslims who lived in the time of the Prophet and witnessed his actions

Isnad The chain of Hadith reporters

Tawatur The chain of Hadith reports

Authority

The Sunnah and Hadith are accepted by all major Islamic schools of thought as authoritative sources. They are not part of the Qur'an or considered sacred like it, but their value has been indispensable for Muslims for centuries.

The Qur'an repeatedly casts Muhammad's authority and guidance as a source of truth and best practice (Qur'an 4: 59, 59: 7). As a result, though they are not a part of the Qur'an as revealed to Muhammad, the Sunnah and Hadith are considered by Muslims to be strongly authoritative sources for Allah's will. The Prophet was also given the task of explaining what had been revealed to him (Qur'an 16: 44), to show the way to a pure life and instruct others in matters of belief (Qur'an 62: 2).

Muhammad has been addressed as 'Ta Ha' (perfect man) (Qur'an 20: 1), and has been presented as 'an excellent model' for believers (Qur'an 33: 21), 'a strong character' (Qur'an 68: 4), 'a light' (Qur'an 5: 15) and 'a mercy ... to all people' (Qur'an 21: 107). Therefore, believers are told to learn from him directly (Qur'an 8: 20) as he was best placed to teach and model the Qur'an (Qur'an 6: 124). For example, while the Qur'an tells Muslims to pray, it does not explain how – this had to be demonstrated by the Prophet. These make the Sunnah and Hadith significant for daily living as Muslims will strive to follow his example.

> When asked to summarise the Prophet, his wife Aishah said: 'The character of the Messenger of Allah was the Qur'an'.

(Muslim, Kitab al-salah, Bab Jami salat al-layl)

> **Now test yourself** TESTED
>
> 6　Why might this statement of Aishah's be used to support the use of the Sunnah and Hadith in addition to the Qur'an?

> [Muhammad] commands them to do right and forbids them to do wrong, who makes good things lawful to them and bad things unlawful.

(Qur'an 7: 157, Haleem 2008)

These teachings suggest that the Sunnah and Hadith are important primary sources in addition to the Qur'an.

> The Qur'an is the foundation of Islam; the Hadith are part of its structural elements. If you start meddling with and dismantling it, you demolish the whole structure.

(Sahib Bleher)

Sira

Sira are early biographies of the Prophet Muhammad and are one of the most important sources about Muhammad's life and the beginnings of Islam. The Sira of historians Ibn Ishaq and Ibn Hisham are among the earliest known and most respected biographies and include many of the key events of Muhammad's life and times, as also found in the Hadith. For example, both Bukhari and Ibn Hisham refer to the first Qur'anic revelation received by the Prophet.

As well as being historically important, the Sira is also considered to be an important religious source. These accounts are less authoritative than the Hadith as the same rigour was not applied to confirm their authenticity, but they are still seen as very valuable.

> I have left two things with you which if you hold on to, you shall not be misguided: the Book of God and my example.

(Hadith, reported by Hakim and Malik)

Suggested answer guidance to exam practice at **www.hoddereducation.co.uk/myrevisionnotesdownloads**

Now test yourself

TESTED ◯

7 How does this quotation: 'I have left two things with you which if you hold on to, you shall not be misguided: the Book of God and my example' show the need for the Sunnah and Hadith?

8 Give two examples from the Qur'an in which Muslims are told to learn from the Prophet.

9 What is the difference between the Hadith and Sira?

Ijma', qiyas and ijtihad

Ijma'

In Islam, ijma' is a consensus of opinion or agreement. This must always be secondary to the primary sources, such as the Qur'an and Hadith, as obeying divine commandments and Muhammad must always come first.

However, if an issue is not directly addressed by the scriptures, the Qur'an gives permission for Muslims to form opinions and make decisions through 'mutual consultation' (Qur'an 42: 38) as long as they are based on the primary sources. This was straightforward while Muhammad was still alive but became more challenging following his death. It was through ijma' that the 'Rightly Guided Caliphs' were elected (see Chapter 6).

As time passed, there was disagreement about whether ijma' included:
+ only the first generation of Muslims
+ the consensus of the first three generations of Muslims (salaf)
+ scholarly consensus (ijma' al-aimmah), the agreement of the jurists (legal experts) and scholars of the whole Muslim world
+ the consensus of all Muslim people (ijma' al-ummah).

> My ummah will never agree upon an error.

(Hadith)

Now test yourself

TESTED ◯

10 How might the Hadith above support ijma' as a source of authority?

Qiyas

Qiyas is a type of reasoning that uses analogies – reaching judgements by applying existing rulings to new situations. Like ijma', this developed out of the main sources. For example, the prohibition of alcohol, which is stated in the Qur'an, was extended to drugs that were not mentioned in the Qur'an but which cause similar intoxicating effects.

This approach, largely adopted by Sunni Muslims, helps apply Islamic principles to ever-changing circumstances. Shi'a Muslims prefer to use a method known as aql (logical reasoning on areas where the Qur'an and Hadith are unclear) and for this to be conducted by descendants of the Prophet Muhammad's family.

Fiqh

As the Islamic empire grew, various interpretations of shari`a were formed. This led to the introduction of the discipline of fiqh ('deep understanding' or 'intelligence', later simply known as Muslim jurisprudence or law). It also led to a number of schools of law developing in both Sunni and Shi'a communities.

The Sunni tradition

In the Sunni tradition these schools of law are known as madhhab and the majority of Sunni Muslims follow one of them. While the schools of law accept the same primary sources and therefore share beliefs and practices, there are some differences between them. For example:

+ Imam Hanifa, Imam Malik and Imam Ahmad all valued local tradition and custom. They believed that as these had been followed by the first Muslims, they must have been closest to Muhammad's Sunnah and handed down by him.
+ Imam Shafi disagreed and felt that following those customs may potentially divert Muslims from the Prophet's way.

> **Madhhab** school of Muslim law

School of law	Founder	Sources used	Popularity
Hanafi	Imam Abu Hanifa (d. 767CE)	Qur'an, Sunnah, ijma' and qiyas	Around a third of all Muslims belong to this school today. Dominant in central Asia, Pakistan, Uzbekistan, Afghanistan, Syria, Jordan and Turkey
Maliki	Imam Malik ibn Anas al-Asbahi (d. 795CE)	Qur'an, Hadiths from people of Madinah	Very popular in Egypt, North Africa and parts of West Africa
Hanbali	Imam Ahmad ibn Hanbal (d. 850CE)	Qur'an, followed by Sunnah	Official school of Saudi Arabia and Qatar, also found in UAE, Iraq and Syria
Shafi	Imam Idris al-Shafi (d. 820CE)	Qur'an, followed by Sunnah, ijma' and qiyas	Scattered all over the Muslim world, particularly East Africa, parts of Egypt and South East Asia

One of the greatest Muslim jurists was Imam Shafi, who studied under Imam Malik. He made a valuable contribution to the development of shari`a by determining the proper use of sources and devising a methodology for fiqh.

The Shi'a tradition

Two main schools of law developed in the Shi'a tradition and they both emphasised that scholars must be from the ahl al-bayt (house, or family, of the Prophet).

> **Ahl al-bayt** house or family of the Prophet Muhammad

School of law	Founder	Popularity
Jafari	Imam Jafar al-Sadiq (d. 765CE)	Popular in Iran, northern Pakistan, central Afghanistan and eastern Iraq. Followed by Twelver Shi'a Muslims (or Ithna Ashariyya)
Zaydiyyah	Named after Zayd ibn Ali (d. 740CE)	Popular in Yemen

Difference of opinion within my community is a sign of the bounty of Allah.

(Hadith)

Another school of law that is neither Sunni nor Shi'a is the Ibadi school which is popular in Oman. The group grew out of the Kharijite movement that opposed the fourth Caliph, Ali, during his leadership.

Ijtihad

The discipline of fiqh – determining laws from primary sources – is a major part of the intellectual struggle known as ijtihad. This is a method of using the principles of the Qur'an, Sunnah and Hadith to identify the best course of action if there is no clear instruction in the sources.

Many Muslim scholars believe that ijtihad is required to help find solutions to new problems. Scholars who are experts in ijtihad are called mujtahids. Here are some examples of contemporary issues that have been resolved using ijtihad:

Mujtahids Experts in ijtihad

+ As mentioned on page 29, many mujtahids concluded that if the effects of using particular drugs are the same or similar to the effects of alcohol, these drugs are included in the Qur'anic prohibition. This is because they would still induce sin, which is forbidden by Allah (Qur'an 7: 33). However, if an intoxicating substance is used in a beneficial way that does not lead to sin (for example, medicinal use) it is permissible.

+ Making interest (riba) on loaned money (usury) is the basis for Western banking but is banned by the Qur'an (3: 130). Some Muslims argue that taking out an interest-bearing loan or mortgage is acceptable because it is unavoidable, while others have worked to create 'sharia-compliant' services through UK or Islamic banks that do not charge interest.

+ Shi'a scholars have varied views on smoking as cigarettes were not available at the time of the Prophet and the Imams (see Chapter 4). Most Sunni scholars consider smoking haram (forbidden) and use the Hadith 'There should be no harm (against oneself) and no harming (against others)' as evidence. The Prophet forbade garlic and onion in mosques due to their smell distracting from worship and many use this argument about smoking too. Muslims who smoke do so despite fatwas (rulings) on this.

Taqlid

Taqlid literally means 'to follow' or 'to imitate' and is used in Shi'a Islam. It refers to following past scholarly authority and opinions as closely as possible. From the time of Muhammad through to their eleventh Imam, Shi'a Muslims were able to receive direct guidance on all matters relating to their faith. They believe that the twelfth Imam was taken by Allah when he was young and will return with Isa (Jesus) near the end of time (see Chapter 4).

In the Imam's absence, Shi'a Muslims follow the decisions made by a mujtahid or faqih (expert in Islamic jurisprudence). For Twelver Shi'as, this is the Marja' Taqlid (source of emulation), better known as the Grand Ayatollah. Their judgements relate to legal and moral matters and not questions of belief.

Opinions regarding traditional and contemporary ijtihad vary:

✔ Ijtihad is essential for Islam to be reformed and modernised. Without it, questions about new issues as they arise would remain unanswered.

✔ The Prophet had said that in each century, a mujaddid (reformer) would be raised by Allah to revive Islam and with the right to reinterpret the sources (Hadith – Abu Daud).

✔ In another Hadith, Muhammad spoke of the Messiah and Mahdi in the future being a 'judge' on religious matters to resolve differences (Hadith – Musnad Ahmad).

✘ The eleventh-century reformer Al-Ghazali declared the gates of ijtihad closed as Muslims no longer had the knowledge and insight to make reinterpretations.

✘ Ijtihad and taqlid were necessary among the earlier generation of Muslims who had the right to use these methods, but this is no longer the case.

✘ Relying on mujtahids to provide rulings can be seen as bid'ah (innovation) and even shirk.

Shirk Setting up partners or equals with Allah

Comparison of approaches on ijtihad

Rashid Rida (1865–1935)	Tariq Ramadan (1962–)
+ Believed the Qur'an, Hadith and accounts of the sahabah were the basis for reform. + Supported reopening ijtihad to make fresh judgements, rather than following traditional scholars unquestioningly. + Rejected taqlid and was disappointed with the poor level of intellectual progress in the Muslim world, seeing the West as more advanced in education and science. + Thought ijtihad was best practised in an Islamic state and supported the revival of the Caliphate.	+ Respects traditional teachings while being open to questioning their relevance today. + Called for a suspension on the use of capital punishment in Muslim countries and promoted debate between scholars to see if particular beliefs and attitudes in Islam are justified today. + Believes Muslims should take pride in their identity and not integrate into non-Muslim societies at the expense of their values.

Chapter summary

+ Shari`a is a code of life that sets out the behaviour and actions expected of Muslims in all circumstances, though there are different views about its application.
+ The primary sources of shari`a are the Qur'an, Sunnah, Hadith and Sira.
+ Muslims also refer to secondary sources including 'ijma, qiyas and ijtihad if further guidance and interpretation is required.

Exam practice

For every syllabus, the higher marks for AO2 (evaluation) come from critical analyis. This means that you will need to be able to do some of the following in your answers:
+ identify the significance
+ evaluate strengths and weaknesses
+ weigh one piece of information against another
+ make reasoned judgements
+ argue a case according to the evidence
+ show why something is relevant or suitable
+ indicate why something will work best
+ identify whether something is appropriate or suitable
+ weigh up the importance of the component parts
+ evaluate the relative significance of details
+ structure information in order of importance
+ show the relevance of links between pieces of information
+ draw conclusions
+ identify why the timing is of importance
+ give the reasons for selecting each option.

Here are some examples of AO2 questions:

'The Hadith are a more reliable source of historical knowledge than the Sira.' Discuss.   [OCR, AO1 and AO2, 30]

'The Qur'an will always be relevant.' Evaluate this view.
[Eduqas, 30]

'The Hadiths have little value as sources of knowledge of the sayings and actions of Muhammad.' Evaluate this view.   [AQA, 15]

Examine the divine nature of the shari`a. [Eduqas/WJEC, 30]

'The doors to ijtihad remain open.' Evaluate this view.
[Eduqas, 30]

A student has started to answer the question below:

'The Qur'an is the only reliable source in Islam.' Evaluate this view.   [Eduqas, 30]

1 Improve the student's answer.
2 Complete the answer by adding a response and an evaluation.

> *Many Muslims would agree with this statement. The Qur'an contains everything Muslims need to know about how to live, and it is also perfect. It states 'We have missed nothing out of the Record' (Qur'an 6: 38), confirming for many Muslims there is nothing missing from the Qur'an in order to know Allah's will and to follow it to the best of their ability. Allah also states that he himself will protect the Qur'an. This has not been said about any other source. This is why Qur'anists reject the Hadith because the same care and attention that went into preserving the Qur'an did not extend to other sources. Furthermore, it is also stated 'Shall I seek any judge other than God, when it is He who has sent down for you [people] the Scripture, clearly explained?' (Qur'an 6: 114). This reinforces the view that everything that Muslims need to know is in the Qur'an.*

4 Beliefs and concepts: articles (Sunni) and roots of faith (Shi'a)

The six articles of faith (Sunni) and five roots of Usul al-Din (Shi'a)

Sunni Islam is based on six articles of faith. Shi'a Muslims follow the five roots of Usul al-Din (principles of faith), which share three of the six articles.

Six articles of faith (Sunni)	Five roots of Usul al-Din (Shi'a)
tawhid – belief in one God, named Allah (see page 34)	
risalah/nubuwwah – belief in all of Allah's prophets and messengers (see page 38)	
akhirah/ma'ad – belief in the afterlife and Day of Judgement (see page 43)	
angels (malaikah) – belief in all the angels of Allah (see page 37)	**imamah** – leadership of the Muslim community by the ahl al-bayt (family of the Prophet Muhammad) (see page 42)
holy books (kutubullah) – belief in and respect for all Islam's sacred texts (see page 39)	**adalat** – divine justice (see page 36)
divine decree about good and evil (Al-Qadr khayrihi washarrihi or just Al-Qadr) – belief that Allah is in control of the outcome of good and evil actions (see page 46)	

The six articles are derived from the Qur'an (Qur'an 2: 177, 4: 136, 57: 22) and the Hadith of Jibril (Gabriel).

> While we were one day sitting with the Messenger of Allah, there appeared before us a man dressed in extremely white clothes and with very black hair. No traces of travel were visible on him, and none of us knew him. He sat down close by the Prophet [... and] he went on to say, 'Inform me about faith'. The Messenger of Allah answered, 'It is that you believe in Allah, and His angels, and His books, and His messengers, and in the Last Day, and in the decree of Allah' [... Later] the man went off. I waited a while, and then the Messenger of Allah said, 'Umar, do you know who that questioner was? [...] That was Jibril (Gabriel). He came to teach you your religion.'

(Hadith – Sahih Muslim, Kitab al-Iman 1: 4)

Belief in these principles is a fundamental requirement in Islam and forms the basis of faith. The articles are interconnected and inform the way Muslims live. Belief in prophets would not be possible without belief in Allah and the angels who reveal his commandments to humanity, which are then recorded in holy books and about which Muslims will be held accountable in the afterlife. These tenets are central to the faith of Muslims.

Allah

'Allah' is the Arabic word for God. It is exclusively his, composed of Al (The) and Ilah (God), and cannot be used for any other deity.

According to Islam, Allah has always existed and is everlasting. As Allah is not a physical being, Muslims believe it is impossible to visualise Him and most consider any attempt to depict him as disrespectful and therefore forbidden.

Attributes of Allah

REVISED

There are two types of attributes:
1 Tanzihi – those that are exclusive to Allah and distinct from creation (e.g. transcendent)
2 Tashbeehi – those that resemble or are shared to some degree by other beings (e.g. forgiving).

According to a Hadith, there are 99 attributes or 'beautiful names' of Allah (7: 180). The Qur'an and Hadith collectively contain more than 100 characteristics of Allah. While these names help to make some sense of his nature, Muslims believe that it is impossible to fully know or describe Allah.

There are some key characteristics of Allah that are emphasised in the Qur'an and Hadith.

Tawhid

REVISED

Tawhid means 'oneness' and is the belief that Allah is unique, indivisible and without any partner.

> *Say, 'He is God the One, God the eternal. He begot no one nor was He begotten. No one is comparable to Him.'*

(Qur'an 112: 1–4, Haleem 2008)

> *Do you not know that control of the heavens and the earth belongs to Him? You [believers] have no protector or helper but God.*

(Qur'an 2: 107, Haleem 2008)

The centrality of tawhid in Muslim belief is further established in the **Shahadah** (Islamic declaration of faith) (see Chapter 5).

Belief in any other form of divinity is ineffective (Qur'an 13: 14) and also shirk, which is the opposite of tawhid and the greatest sin in Islam. This is why Muhammad preached that people should worship one God only. Therefore, tawhid is a statement of uncompromising monotheism.

Seyyed Hossein Nasr says that the two meanings of tawhid are:
+ the oneness of God
+ unity in creation, including between human beings and other creatures of God.

> **Tawhid** Belief in the oneness of Allah. The oneness and unity of Allah
>
> **Shahadah** Declaration of faith

Allah as creator

REVISED

Because Allah is the only God, Muslims believe that he is the sole creator of everything.

> *(He is) the Creator of the heavens and earth. He made mates for you from among yourselves – and for the animals too – so that you may multiply. There is nothing like Him: He is the All Hearing, the All Seeing.*

(Qur'an 42: 11, Haleem 2008)

Allah as immanent and transcendent

REVISED

Muslims believe that Allah is both near and far. Humans can observe and experience some parts of Allah's creation, but much of it is beyond their understanding.

One belief about Allah is that he is immanent which means that although Allah acts throughout the universe, he remains close to humans:

We are closer to him than his jugular vein.

(Qur'an 50: 16, Haleem 2008)

Another belief is that he is transcendent, which means that he is above and beyond creation:

No vision can take Him in, but He takes in all vision. He is the All Subtle, the All Aware.

(Qur'an 6: 103, Haleem 2008)

> **Exam tip**
>
> Don't confuse Immanent with imminent – they sound the same and have similar meanings as they both refer to closeness, but make sure you use the right one! One way of remembering this is to think of Immanent having the letter A in it – A for Allah.

Allah as omnipotent

REVISED

Muslims believe that Allah is omnipotent, meaning 'all powerful'. This means that he has the power to create everything from nothing and can do as he wills. He is the only authority in the universe.

Your Lord is God, who created the heavens and earth in six Days, then established Himself on the throne.

(Qur'an 7: 54, Haleem 2008)

In this verse, the Qur'an refers to Allah seating himself 'on the throne', which many Muslims understand as symbolic of his control over everything. It can also signify knowledge. This is further highlighted in ayat al-kursi, known in English as the Throne Verse. Muhammad referred to it as the 'loftiest verse' in the Qur'an.

Allah as merciful and compassionate

REVISED

Allah is described as compassionate and his kindness knows no limits: 'Your Lord's bounty is not restricted.' (Qur'an 17: 20). This includes responding to those who are distressed and turn to him for help (Qur'an 27: 62).

The Qur'an mentions mercy as one of Allah's principal attributes. The tasmiyyah, 'In the name of God, Most Gracious, Most Merciful' appears in the Qur'an 114 times.

My mercy embraces all things.

(Qur'an 7: 156, Haleem 2008)

> **Revision activity**
>
> Write a short paragraph explaining how belief in Allah as omnipotent and merciful may influence a Muslim's life.

The Prophet said:

A person will be brought before God Almighty, and He will place His arm around him and say: 'Did you commit such-and-such sin?'

He will submit, 'Yes.'

Then God Almighty will ask: 'Did you commit such-and-such sin?'

He will say, 'Yes.'

Then God Almighty will make him confess [all of his sins] and will say, 'I concealed your sins for you in the world, and today I shall forgive them all.'

(Hadith – Bukhari, Kitab al-Adab, 6070)

Understanding Allah's merciful nature inspires Muslims to want to be thankful and establish a close relationship with him. This is expressed through worship, which, according to the Qur'an, is the very reason that humans were created (Qur'an 51: 56). Practices such as Salah (see Chapter 5) help Muslims to develop gratitude for Allah's benevolence.

Many Muslims pray by addressing Allah by the attributes that are relevant to what is being prayed for. For instance, someone with financial worries may focus on Allah's attribute of being the Provider. This is another way human purpose is achieved. William Chittick says that reflection on God's attributes teaches Muslims that he is the source and sustainer of everything.

Meditating on God's Quranic Names leads to the understanding that everything in the universe comes from God, returns to God, and is sustained and supported by God at every moment.

Allah as just

REVISED

For Shi'a Muslims, Allah's attribute of Al-Adl (The Just) is particularly important as adalat (divine justice) is one of the five roots of Usul al-Din. Adalat teaches that believers are accountable for what they have and have not done. As a reflection of this divine characteristic, Allah also expects people to show fairness in everything they do (Qur'an 7: 29).

Some consider the concept of adalat problematic as it implies that Allah must always punish sinners. This appears to contradict the belief in his limitless mercy. Responses to this include:

+ Allah is not like a judge who is bound to deal with people according to their deeds. He is Master of his own law, which means that he can choose to be merciful if he wishes.
+ Everything Allah does should be seen as an act of mercy and compassion, including punishment, as punishment can correct our ways.
+ Some Muslims believe that hell is not forever so even those whom Allah punishes will be shown mercy and will enter heaven once they have paid for their sins (Qur'an 39: 53, Hadith – Kanzul Ummal).

Questions about the nature of Allah

REVISED

Although Muslims all share a belief in these attributes of Allah, there are still some questions about whether his nature is coherent:

+ How can Allah have so many characteristics and still be one being?
+ How can Allah be both merciful and just?

Muslims believe that just as human beings have multiple qualities – for example, the capacity to be kind and loyal – so does Allah, but at a supreme level.

Now test yourself

TESTED

And, with full knowledge, for We were never far from them, We shall tell them what they did.

(Qur'an 7: 7, Haleem 2008)

If My servants ask you about Me, I am near. I respond to those who call Me.

(Qur'an 2: 186, Haleem 2008)

1 Choose one of these quotes and explain in your own words what they teach about Allah's attributes.
2 Give two reasons why the attributes of Allah are important for Muslims.
3 How do Muslims believe it is possible to believe in a God who cannot be understood fully? Explain your answer.

Suggested answer guidance to exam practice at **www.hoddereducation.co.uk/myrevisionnotesdownloads**

Angels

The nature of angels

Muslims hold angels, known in Arabic as malaikah, in high reverence and say 'peace be upon him' after any angel is mentioned.

Muslims believe that angels have no free will and can only obey Allah's commands, which makes them different from humans. The angels all bowed down to Adam, meaning they were made to serve him (Qur'an 20: 116).

They do not speak before He speaks and they act by His command.

(Qur'an 21: 27, Haleem 2008)

The nature of angels cannot be fully known, leading to varying opinions about them. The Qur'an says that angels have appointed stations (Qur'an 37: 164–5), meaning that they work in their respective spheres and carry out the responsibilities assigned to them (Qur'an 66: 6). Many Muslims believe that they do not possess any fixed material form, but that they can still be identified by people when they appear to them (such as in a vision). For instance, it is believed the angel Jibril (Gabriel) appeared to Isa (Jesus) in the form of a dove and to Muhammad as an ordinary human being.

The role of angels

Angels are intermediaries between Allah and his creation. Their important roles include:

+ giving people strength in times of need and assuring them of heavenly support (Qur'an 41: 30–32)
+ protecting individuals and recording their deeds, carried out by 'noble scribes', known in Arabic as Al-Kiram Al-Katibun (Qur'an 82: 10–12, Qur'an 54: 53)
+ supporting believers during times of war, such as the battles in early Islam (Qur'an 3: 125–7)
+ accompanying the souls of people to the next life.

> **Exam tip**
>
> The role of angels conveying God's messages to humanity can be compared to that of a postal worker delivering a letter from the writer to the addressee.

Now test yourself TESTED

4 How might these examples affect the way Muslims live their life?

There is a hierarchy among angels. The highest-ranking ones are called 'archangels'. These include Jibril, Mika'il and Israfil.

Jibril (Gabriel)

Jibril has a unique role. He is also called 'the Holy Spirit' (Qur'an 16: 102) and 'The Trustworthy Spirit' (Qur'an 26: 193). Muslims believe that Jibril is the messenger of revelation between Allah and his prophets and delivered the entire Qur'an to Muhammad.

Jibril also:
+ taught Muhammad how to pray and showed him heaven
+ sometimes appeared to Muhammad in the form of a man and was observed by others, such as the time Jibril walked in as a stranger asking Muhammad about Islam. This was a means for teaching Muslims about their faith (Hadith)
+ descends during Laylat al-Qadr (the Night of Power)
+ visited Muhammad every night in Ramadan to teach him the Qur'an and did this twice in the last year of the Prophet's life.

Shi'a Muslims believe that he also visited much of the ahl al-bayt, including Ali and Fatimah (Muhammad's daughter and Ali's wife).

Mika'il (Michael)

REVISED

Mika'il's role is to take care of the provision and maintenance of life. He is believed to be in charge of plants and the rain, which many Muslims have interpreted more generally to mean that he provides food for the body and soul. Like Jibril, Mika'il is mentioned by name in the Qur'an (2: 98).

Other beliefs about Mika'il include how he accompanied Jibril and Israfil, and visited Ibrahim to inform him that his wife would have a son and also warned about the destruction of the people of Lot.

Israfil (Uriel)

In the Qur'an, Israfil is mentioned as being the angel who blows a trumpet, first to announce the end of time and secondly to announce the Day of Judgement.

> **Now test yourself** TESTED
>
> 5 'In Islam, Jibril is the most important of all angels.' Write at least one point for and one against this statement.

Revelation (wahy) and the role and nature of prophets

Muslims believe that one of the reasons that humans were created is to worship Allah (Qur'an 51: 56). As part of this, the two most fundamental duties of all Muslims are to fulfil the rights of Allah (Huquq Allah) and the rights of his creation including humanity (Huquq al-`Ibad).

According to the Qur'an, Allah appoints prophets to receive wahy (revelation) to communicate his will to humans.

> It is not granted to any mortal that God should speak to him except through revelation [wahy], or from **behind a veil**, or by **sending a messenger** to reveal by His command what He will: He is exalted and wise.

(Qur'an 42: 51, Haleem 2008)

As with angels, prophets are given great respect and Muslims say 'peace be upon him' after their names. In Arabic, prophecy or the system of prophethood is known as nubuwwah. A prophet is called nabi, which also means someone who gives news. The Qur'an uses other titles for prophets:

+ rasul (messenger)
+ nadir (warner)
+ caliph (successor)
+ imam (leader).

All prophets have the same role. Their purpose is to:

+ strengthen belief in tawhid (Qur'an 16: 36)
+ give glad tidings to believers and warnings to non-believers (Qur'an 4: 165)
+ purify people (Qur'an 62: 2)
+ establish justice (Qur'an 57: 25)
+ resolve disputes between people (Qur'an 2: 213) and unite humanity (Qur'an 49: 13)
+ separate the wicked from the community of believers (Qur'an 3: 179)
+ provide proof of Allah's existence through prayer, miracles and other signs (Qur'an 4: 165)
+ act as moral examples and an inspiration for Muslims.

Wahy: the words of Allah brought directly to an individual.

Behind a veil: Allah's order is brought to an individual through a kashf (vision), ruya (dream) or a piece of text that comes into view.

Sending of a messenger: the appearance, usually of an angel, speaking on behalf of God. This is possible whether the person is awake or asleep.

Nubuwwah Prophethood

Nabi Prophet

Prophets in Islam also have characteristics that differentiate them from figures in other religions:

+ They have limited knowledge and don't claim to know everything.
+ They cannot be guilty of sin (Qur'an 3: 161).
+ They are mortal and cannot return from the dead.

The Prophet Muhammad said that Allah has sent 124,000 prophets to the world. Muslims must believe in all of them. Each prophet is sent to pass on messages from Allah to people living in their particular time and location, which is the reason why so many have been sent. They are also required to take a covenant from people that they will believe in and support the next prophet who appears (Qur'an 3: 81).

Many of these messages have been recorded in ancient scriptures (kutubullah). The six articles of faith requires that holy books from the time before Islam must be respected by Muslims as they were originally from Allah and the Qur'an confirms many of the previous revelations. Nubuwwah is also included in the Shi'a five roots of Usul al-Din.

> **Kutubullah** Holy books

The Qur'an mentions the names of at least 25 prophets, including the founding figures of the Abrahamic religious traditions, namely Ibrahim (Abraham), Musa (Moses) and Isa (Jesus). All prophets have been men due to men and women having distinct roles in society (see Chapter 9).

Nabi and rasul

Muslims believe that some prophets were given a new message or law to replace an earlier one. This would happen if previous guidance had become unreliable or irrelevant because circumstances had changed.

There is disagreement among Muslims about whether there is a difference between a nabi (prophet) and rasul (messenger). Here are some of the arguments on both sides.

> **Exam tip**
>
> Remember that the plural of nabi is anbiya and the plural of rasul is rusul.

Different	Not different
+ A Hadith states that there have been 124,000 anbiya and 313 rusul + All rusul are anbiya but not all anbiya are rusul + Rusul are given a new religious law (shari`a) and message, while anbiya continue a previous one + Rusul and anbiya are mentioned separately in the Qur'an (Qur'an 22: 52) + The Qur'an refers to the need to believe in rusul specifically, along with other articles of faith (Qur'an 2: 285)	+ This Hadith has been classified as da'if (weak) and therefore unreliable + The two terms are interchangeable – all anbiya are rusul and vice versa + Not all rusul bring new laws – both Ismai'l and Isa are called rasul (Qur'an 19: 54, 61: 6) but followed a previous shari`a + Prophets can have multiple descriptions – rasul and nabi are two aspects of the same role: rasul for receiving a divine message and nabi for passing it on + Anbiya are included in this belief. Muhammad's description as 'Seal of the Prophets' (anbiya) also means 'Seal of the Messengers' (rusul) + Belief in rusul (messengers) is stated as a fundamental belief (Qur'an 2: 285) and this must include all anbiya (prophets).

Islam and other Abrahamic faiths

Many key figures from other Abrahamic faiths are regarded as prophets in Islam. Muslim beliefs about these prophets have many similarities with Jewish and Christian beliefs, but there are also some differences.

Adam

REVISED

+ Believed to be the first prophet. Also called Allah's caliph (deputy/vice general), whom the angels had to serve.
+ Considered by most Muslims also to be the first man, but by a minority of Muslims as part of the first civilisation of human beings (see Chapter 7).
+ Lived with his wife Hawwa (Eve) in a beautiful garden. Both were told to enjoy its comforts and also commanded to keep away from a 'tree' which represented evil, but they were deceived by Satan. This resulted in them both being ejected from the garden. This is similar to the description of Adam in the book of Genesis. However, while Genesis describes Adam's actions as humanity's first sin, Muslims believe it is impossible for a prophet to commit any sin and that Adam simply made a mistake (Qur'an 2: 36).
+ Highly regarded because Allah chose him over all the people of his time (Qur'an 3: 33) and treated him with great mercy.

Ibrahim (Abraham)

REVISED

+ Called the 'father of the prophets', Allah's 'friend' (Qur'an 4: 125) and the 'first Muslim'.
+ One of the Prophet Muhammad's ancestors.
+ Rejected idolatry and was thrown into fire by his enemies but survived.
+ Presented as an example of obedience and faith (Qur'an 16: 120).
+ Had two sons Ishaq (Isaac) and Isma'il (Ishmael) who were also prophets.
+ Saw a dream that he was sacrificing Isma'il. When Ibrahim shared the dream with him, Isma'il did not hesitate and was ready to give his life. Just as Ibrahim was about to sacrifice Isma'il, God called out to him to stop and praised them both for their spirit of dedication. This event is commemorated at Id-ul-Adha (see Chapter 5).
+ Rebuilt the Ka`bah with Isma'il.
+ Given the Sahifa (Scrolls), one of the earliest known divine texts – now believed to be lost (Qur'an 87: 19).

Musa (Moses)

REVISED

+ The main prophet of Judaism.
+ Mentioned more times in the Qur'an than anyone else.
+ Had a brother, Harun (Aaron), who was also a prophet.
+ Freed the Israelites from slavery under the harsh rule of the Fir'awn (Pharaoh) in Egypt.
+ Performed many miracles, like the parting of the seas to allow the Israelites to escape (Qur'an 26: 52–68).
+ Given the Tawrat (Torah) by God. Muslims believe that this became distorted while scribes were composing the books from memory 1,000 years after Musa. Despite this, Muslims still consider the Tawrat to be an important text and believe that it includes a prophecy about the future appearance of the Prophet Muhammad: 'I will raise them up a Navi [Prophet] from among their achim [brothers], like unto thee, and will put My words in his mouth.' (Deuteronomy 18: 18 – Orthodox Jewish Bible).

Dawud (David)

REVISED ●

+ One of the Israelite prophets after Musa.
+ Remembered for his wisdom, prayers and fasting, as well as for his victory against the oppressive Jalut (Goliath), after which he was made king of the Israelites, signifying both spiritual and worldly honour (Qur'an 2: 251).
+ Given the Zabur (Psalms) containing songs, prayers and poems, which Muslims believe were inspired by Allah (Qur'an 17: 55).

Isa (Jesus)

REVISED ●

+ Among the most honoured prophets of Allah.
+ Frequently named in the Qur'an and Hadith along with his mother Maryam (Mary).
+ Famous for many miracles, including his own birth which did not involve a biological father. He is also attributed with creating birds out of clay and bringing the dead back to life (Qur'an 3: 49), although many Muslims understand these acts to have a symbolic meaning (for example, bringing people out of darkness and into light).
+ Was not divine, God's literal son or killed on the cross according to the Qur'an, but saved (Qur'an 4: 157–8).
+ Foretold the coming of a prophet after him named 'Ahmad' (understood to mean Muhammad) (Qur'an 61: 6).
+ Given the Injil (the Gospel) – not to be confused with the four gospels in the Christian New Testament, parts of which Muslims believe are unreliable. Muslims believe that much of the Injil of Isa became lost, forgotten or altered.
+ Sunni and Shi'a Muslims believe that Isa remains physically alive and will come to Earth again near the Day of Judgement with the Imam Mahdi (guided leader) to restore justice and to defeat al-Masih ad-Dajjal (the Antichrist). Ahmadiyya Muslims believe that Isa has passed away (Qur'an 5: 116–117, 3: 144) and so cannot return. Instead, a messiah born in the ummah, who is also the Mahdi, would lead a spiritual, not physical battle against evil. They believe their nineteenth-century founder Mirza Ghulam Ahmad was this promised figure.

> **Revision activity**
>
> Create a Venn diagram comparing Christian and Muslim views about Isa (Jesus).

The Prophet Muhammad

Muhammad has a special role in Islam because Muslims believe that:
+ he was the only prophet to have been given a universal message for all times
+ he is described in the Qur'an as 'Ta Ha' (perfect man) (Qur'an 20: 1), been described as having 'a strong character' (Qur'an 68: 4), 'a light' (Qur'an 5: 15) and 'a mercy... to all people' (Qur'an 21: 107)
+ he was unique among all prophets and messengers, praised for being 'an excellent model' (Qur'an 33: 21) – the exemplar of how to live for people at all levels (personal, family, social, moral, political and religious)
+ he personified all qualities – humility, patience, forgiveness, justice – in all situations (for example, times of persecution and authority) as a lesson for all people
+ his Sunnah and the Hadith are important sources of authority, second only to the Qur'an (see Chapter 3)
+ he is included in a special prayer, repeated by Muslims many times every day, asking Allah to bless him and the ummah (Qur'an 33: 56)
+ he was given the Qur'an along with its correct understanding and implementation (Qur'an 3: 164).

Khatam an-Nabiyyin (Seal of the Prophets)

REVISED ○

The Qur'an refers to Muhammad as Khatam an-Nabiyyin – 'Seal of the Prophets' (Qur'an 33: 40). This is because he was given the final scripture and shari'ah that was never to change or be replaced. Generally, the term is also understood to mean that Muhammad is the last in the line of prophets and messengers beginning with Adam.

Another reading of 'Seal of the Prophets' is that all the qualities found in every prophet and messenger found their perfect expression in Muhammad, and that he attested to the truth of all other prophets. This confirms the relationship between Islam and earlier Abrahamic faiths (Qur'an 10: 37).

According to Ahmadiyya Muslims, the word 'Khatam' refers to the highest level a person may reach in their field that cannot be surpassed. Therefore, as Khatam al-Nabiyyin, Muhammad was the master prophet and chief of all the messengers. According to their interpretation of Qur'an 4: 69 and 22: 75, it is also possible for an ummati (follower) prophet to appear who would be under the authority of the Qur'an and the Prophet Muhammad. Many Muslims do not recognise Ahmadiyya Muslims as part of Islam, although the Ahmadiyya self-identify as Muslims.

Exam tip

This is an example of disagreement between Muslims about the meaning of a part of the Qur'an.

What is the Imamah?

You who believe, obey God and the Messenger, and those in authority among you. If you are in dispute over any matter, refer it to God and the Messenger, if you truly believe in God and the Last Day: that is better and fairer in the end.

(Qur'an 4: 59, Haleem 2008)

Shi'a Muslims believe that Imamah (leadership) is particularly important and that is the reason why it is among the five roots of Usul al-Din.

The Imamate includes all prophets from Adam to Muhammad. Following the death of Muhammad, the title of Imam was conferred on the people who Shi'a Muslims believe to be his rightful successors. There is a strict criteria for this, for instance, they must be from the ahl al-bayt (the family of Muhammad) and be granted divine knowledge and authority ('ismah). Imams are not prophets but are the closest to them spiritually.

Imamah Succession or leadership of the Prophet's family (Shi'a)

What do Shi'a Muslims believe about Imams?

REVISED ○

Shi'a Muslims believe that the title 'Imam' only applies to members of the ahl al-bayt, designated as perfect, pure and infallible by the preceding Imam under divine inspiration (nass).

They believe that Imams have divine protection and cannot be surpassed in their piety, knowledge and wisdom ('ilm).

Exam tip

Remember this is different from the Sunni Rightly Guided Caliphate (Khilafah) where leaders were chosen or elected from the Muslim community by consensus (ijma' – see Chapter 3).

Caliphate System of succession or leadership following the Prophet Muhammad (Sunni)

What does an Imam do?

Imams provide commentary on and interpretation of the Qur'an and guidance to the ummah. This guardianship is known as wilayah. They are believed to be the means through which people receive divine grace on account of their obedience to Allah.

> We are the ones to whom God has made obedience obligatory. The people will not prosper unless they recognise us and the people will not be excused if they are ignorant of us.

(Ja'far al-Sadiq, the Sixth Imam)

What are different Shi'a beliefs about Imamate?

+ The largest group of Shi'a Muslims, the Ithna Ash`ari (Twelvers), believe that there have been twelve imams since Muhammad.
+ There was a split following the death of the sixth Imam, Ja'far al-Sadiq, as to who should have been the next Imam.
+ The Twelvers believe it was Musa Al-Kadhim, while others believe it was Isma'il. These are known as Isma'ili Shi'a Muslims, sometimes referred to as Seveners.
+ Twelvers believe the succession of Imams continued until the occultation (disappearance) of the twelfth Imam, Muhammad Al-Mahdi, who is still alive somewhere in the world and will one day emerge and bring equality to all.
+ In his absence, Twelver Shi'a Muslims derive guidance from ayatollahs who have spent many years studying Islamic theology and so are seen as experts in the faith.
+ Nizari and Musta'li Isma'ili Muslims believe the succession continued through their seventh Imam Isma'il but the Imamate was no longer hereditary. Each Imam chose his successor. The largest Isma'ili group are the Naziri Isma'ilis whose current leader is Mawlana Hazar Imam.

Resurrection and afterlife

The belief in life after death

The Qur'an refers to righteous people as those who 'believe in the Unseen' and those who have faith in Allah and the 'Last Day' (Qur'an 2: 3–8). These expressions signify the great importance of the belief in life after death.
+ For Sunni Muslims, this belief is the akhirah and is one of the six articles of faith.
+ For Shi'a Muslims, it is referred to as ma'ad and is one of the five roots of Usul al-Din.

Muslims are conscious that everyone's time on Earth is limited and so they must live morally in submission to the will of Allah. This is the purpose of life and has important implications for what happens after death. Intentions and actions on Earth are recorded by the noble scribes Al-Kiram Al-Katibun, and are then taken into account at the time of judgement.

A prayer that Muslims often recite is:

> Our Lord, give us good in this world and in the Hereafter, and protect us from the torment of the Fire.

(Qur'an 2: 201, Haleem 2008)

Free will

Islam teaches that every individual has free will and will be held responsible for their deeds. The Qur'an refers to three types of human self or soul:

1 **Nafs al-ammarah** – the self that is prone to evil (Qur'an 12: 53). This is the lowest state of a person: they are frequently inclined towards wrongdoing.
2 **Nafs al-lawwamah** – the self that reproves (Qur'an 75: 2). This is the middle state of a person: they are able to make rational decisions but are not free from committing sins.
3 **Nafs al-mutma'innah** – the self at peace (Qur'an 89: 27). This is the highest state: they become spiritually pure and establish a lasting relationship with God.

Afterlife

According to the Qur'an, the afterlife is a certainty:

> It is God who gives you life, then causes you to die, and then He gathers you all to the Day of Resurrection of which there is no doubt, though most people do not comprehend.

(Qur'an 45: 26, Haleem 2008)

The Qur'an also addresses any criticism of the afterlife (Qur'an 36: 78–81), arguing that:

+ all prophets have taught about it
+ societies built on this belief are more peaceful and commit less evil
+ rejection of this belief has led to nations being punished
+ people's sense of morality and justice demands that everyone is accountable for their actions which does not always happen in this life
+ life has no purpose unless there is continued existence in another world.

Muslims believe that the soul is immortal. It is not only taken by Allah at the time of death but also during sleep (Qur'an 39: 54). Following our physical death, we will be raised again in the next life. The Qur'an refers to three stages of human existence:

1 **This world** – whatever a person does in their lifetime is recorded and cannot be altered afterwards.
2 **Barzakh** (meaning barrier) – the intermediate state between death and judgement, when the soul has left the body. Beliefs about this stage include:
   + Once the soul is separated from the body no progress or improvements to one's past life can be made.
   + A person will be questioned about their deeds, which will affect their experience in Barzakh. Reward and punishment start immediately.
   + The soul is provided a new body that is either bright or dark depending on the lightness or darkness of its deeds. Pure souls will be bright, indicating they will go to heaven, and the impure will be being dark indicating they will go to hell.
   + The soul waits until the next stage, already knowing what its fate will be.
3 **Resurrection** – when all graves will be opened and each person will be given another body that will see and know Allah.

Israfil first blows the trumpet on the Final Day when the entirety of creation will be destroyed. He blows it a second time at resurrection. Some consider this resurrection to be physical and believe this is why bodies need to be buried and remain in graves until judgement. Most Muslims say that dead bodies are buried out of respect and it is just the soul that is taken away and provided with a new form in the afterlife.

44

Judgement

Yawm al-Qiyama (the Day of Resurrection) is believed to be Allah's final assessment of humanity. Yawm ad-Din (the Day of Judgement) and Yawm al-Akhirah (the Last Day) are other terms used for this event.

The time of the event is not specified, but the Hadiths outline the signs that it is imminent:

+ the prevalence of corruption and conflict in the world
+ the appearance of the al-Masih ad-Dajjal (the Anti-Christ), who will be defeated by Isa and the Mahdi
+ followed by a period of serenity before the end of the world, the beginning of resurrection and judgement.

Not all Muslims accept this literal reading and argue that it is symbolic of the desperate state of the world and humanity's last chance to turn to Allah.

Muslims believe that Allah is omniscient and therefore his judgement will always be right and fair. For Shi'a Muslims, this links to adalat. Allah's mercy can be requested by special individuals (intercession). For Sunni Muslims this individual can only be Muhammad, while for Shi'a Muslims it can be anyone in the ahl al-bayt (Prophet's family).

> The Hadith say that there are three things that continue to benefit a believer even after death:
>
> 1 charity which they had given (which continues to benefit others)
> 2 beneficial knowledge which they had left behind
> 3 supplication on their behalf by a righteous child.

Heaven

Heaven or paradise (Jannah in Arabic) is described in the Qur'an as a beautiful place where people may enjoy various rewards. Many passages appear to refer to material things being provided in the afterlife.

> Here is a picture of the Garden promised to the pious: rivers of water forever pure, rivers of milk forever fresh, rivers of wine, a delight for those who drink, rivers of honey clarified and pure, [all] flow in it; there they will find fruit of every kind; and they will find forgiveness from their Lord. How can this be compared to the fate of those stuck in the Fire, given boiling water to drink that tears their bowels?

(Qur'an 47: 15, Haleem 2008)

The reference to 'rivers of wine' has raised questions as alcohol is prohibited in the Qur'an (5: 90–1). It has been explained that the wine in heaven does not intoxicate (Qur'an 37: 47) and is 'a pure drink' (Qur'an 76: 21). This shows that the meaning of a word depends on the context in which it is used.

In other places, comparisons are made between this life and the next to show that life after death is based on what we experience on Earth. Believers are promised 'two gardens' (Qur'an 55: 46), one in this life, one in the next.

Many Muslims believe that life in heaven is not static but a continuous journey towards higher levels of progress towards Allah.

Hell

In contrast to heaven, hell (Jahannam) is described as a place of pain and suffering for people who did not live moral lives and chose to reject the prophets sent to them (Qur'an 67: 6–11).

Some Muslims believe that the graphic descriptions of hell as a fiery place of torture, where sinners are chained, made to drink boiling water, eat scalding food and choke columns of fire, are literally true. Some Muslims consider much of the Qur'an's language to be symbolic and believe that the ways in which hell is portrayed are intended to highlight the danger of not believing in Allah and to deter people from committing sins.

Many Muslims believe that hell, like heaven, is the final destination for those Allah decides to place there. Other Muslims argue that hell is only temporary, as Allah is Al-Ghafur (forgiving) and will eventually admit people to heaven.

My servants who have harmed yourselves by your own excess, do not despair of God's mercy. God forgives all sins: He is truly the Most Forgiving, the Most Merciful.

(Qur'an 39: 53, Haleem 2008)

> **Now test yourself**   TESTED ●
>
> 6 'A time will come in hell when not a single man would be left in it. Its doors and windows will rattle to the blowing wind.' (Hadith – Kanzul Ummal)
>   How does this Hadith about the afterlife link to beliefs about the attributes of Allah?
>
> 7 'Akhirah gives life a purpose.' Write down two supporting statements from a Muslim perspective.
>
> 8 Do you think Muslim teachings about the Day of Judgement and afterlife might inspire fear or faith? Write a statement explaining your view.

Divine decree and free will

Divine decree

'Divine decree' is usually referred to as Al-Qadr khayrihi washarrihi (Al-Qadr for short) or predestination and is the belief that Allah is in control of the outcome of good and evil actions.

Allah is believed to be omnipotent (all-powerful) and omniscient (all-knowing). This means that he already knows everything that will happen. This is written in the Al-Lawh al-Mahfuz (the Preserved Tablet) in the heavens.

The Qur'an describes how Allah has predetermined many things, from how the cosmos should work: 'He has subjected the sun and the moon each to pursue its course for an appointed time' (Qur'an 13: 2) to the deaths of every individual: 'No soul may die except with God's permission at a predestined time' (Qur'an 3: 145).

Human free will

At the same time, humans are given the capacity to make many choices about their actions. For instance, if a person is hungry and has food in front of them, they have the choice to eat straightaway or to wait until later.

Freedom applies in religious matters too. While Islam has been declared to be Allah's chosen religion (Qur'an 5: 3), no one can be forced to believe in it (Qur'an 2: 256).

> Say, 'Now the truth has come from your Lord: let those who wish to believe in it do so, and let those who wish to reject it do so.'

(Qur'an 18: 29, Haleem 2008)

> Do the believers not realize that if God had so willed, He could have guided all mankind?

(Qur'an 13: 31, Haleem 2008)

There is also a distinction between what Allah wills and what he permits. People's intentions, decisions and actions are recorded by Al-Kiram Al-Katibun and will be read out on the Day of Judgement when people will be held accountable for their choices fairly.

Reconciling divine decree and free will

A key question at the heart of these beliefs is, if Allah has control over everything in the universe, how is it possible for human beings to have freedom?

According to the Qur'an, every person is free to choose how they act. At the same time, there are some things that are predetermined and unchangeable. These are part of the Sunnah (practice) of Allah. For Muslims, this shows that Allah's laws and personal freedom can be reconciled to bring about a certain outcome, which forms part of Al-Qadr and a bigger divine plan.

Scholars have identified two types of divine decree:
1 **Mu'allaq** – decrees that can be averted by prayer, repentance, humility and almsgiving, as long as they do not conflict with divine laws
2 **Mubram** – decrees that cannot be changed by anything, including prayers and almsgiving, as they are part of a predetermined plan, like the law of gravity.

Therefore, a prayer asking Allah for the recovery of a sick relative may be granted but praying to be transported back in time would not.

Sunni and Shi'a Muslim beliefs about the nature of predestination are broadly similar but there are minor differences:
+ Sunni Muslims believe that everything that is to happen is already predetermined, known and unalterable by Allah.
+ Shi'a Muslims believe in the concept of Bada' which states that Allah can change a person's destiny according to their actions.

Despite Allah being transcendent and therefore not completely knowable, both Sunni and Shi'a Islam consider divine control and human freedom to be perfectly compatible. These beliefs have been influenced by two groups from the early period of Islam, Mu'tazili and Ash`ari, between the eighth and tenth centuries CE.

47

Mu`tazili	Ash`ari
Rationalist school of Islam that flourished in what is now Iraq and made a significant impact on Shi'a theology	Sunni school founded by Abu al-Hasan al-Ash`ari who separated from his Mu`tazilite teachers and companions
+ Humans must have total free will. Allah is benevolent and does not cause or want evil, but it exists due to humanity. The view that humans have complete freedom is known as libertarianism + Allah allows human suffering as a moral test and does not burden people beyond their capacity (Qur'an 2: 286) + Actions are either good or evil – Allah must honour his promise to reward virtue and punish sin + Reward and punishment is just if humans truly have freedom + Passages in the Qur'an about Allah guiding and leading people astray (Qur'an 14: 4) refer to the Day of Judgement, not this life	+ Humans have complete free will (ikhtiyar) and some freedom of action, but do not have the power to create actions – they are themselves makhluq (created) while only Allah is khaliq (creator) and is the cause of everything. This view is known as occasionalism + Humans cannot truly understand ideas about freedom and justice – these are known to Allah alone + God's judgement is right and fair, even if a human's limited understanding might make it seem the opposite + Sinners may be forgiven in hell

A key member of the Ash`ari school was Abu Hamid Al-Ghazali, the eleventh-century Muslim reformer. In the Jerusalem Epistle he wrote on the nature of divine decree and humanity's free will. He stated that Allah's perfect and unchanging nature and his omnipotence and omniscience meant that if all mankind, jinn and angels worked together to affect a single particle without Allah's will, they would be unable to.

He also criticised the Mu`tazilis libertarian approach to human free will:
+ Human freedom is an illusion; no human is able to do whatever they wish.
+ Everything came into existence by the act of God. This includes all favours and benefits on human beings. Nothing Allah does can be wrong or unjust.
+ Prophets have been sent to show signs about Allah's truth and it is every human being's responsibility to recognise this.
+ Mu`tazilis are wrong to believe Allah does what is in people's best interests as he is the cause and master of everything.

In late nineteenth-century India, a disagreement arose between two prominent figures, Sir Sayyed Ahmad Khan and Mirza Ghulam Ahmad on the nature of predestination, particularly with reference to prayer. Ultimately, most Muslims believe that Allah hears and accepts the prayers of believers which are offered in humility and sincerity, and that their acceptance sets in motion a chain of causes which can lead to the fulfilment of the objective that was prayed for. This also constitutes part of divine decree.

Chapter summary

+ The core beliefs of Muslims are encapsulated in the six articles of faith (Sunni) and five roots of Usul al-Din (Shi'a)
+ The centrality of belief in the oneness of Allah, prophethood and the afterlife are shared by Sunni and Shi'a Muslims.
+ The beliefs are interconnected and influence the way Muslims live their life in private and in public.

Exam practice

Explain the nature and purpose of angels in Islam. [WJEC, AO1, 15]

Examine Muslim beliefs about the akhirah. [AQA, AO1, 10]

To what extent are revelation and prophecy central beliefs in Islam? [OCR, AO1 and AO2, 30]

Analyse the relationship between tawhid, the 99 names of Allah and adalat. [Pearson Edexcel, AO1 and AO2, 20]

'Muhammad was the ideal prophet and messenger.' Evaluate this view. [Eduqas, AO2, 30]

Suggested answer guidance to exam practice at **www.hoddereducation.co.uk/myrevisionnotesdownloads**

5 Practices and identity

The foundations of Islam: Five Pillars (Sunni) and Ten Obligatory Acts (Shi'a)

All religions have a firm foundation setting out the key duties of their adherents. This foundation differs slightly between Sunni and Shi'a Islam.

In Sunni Islam this foundation is known as the Five Pillars which, like columns in a building, support the main principles and practices of the faith, and shape and express Muslim identity. They are:

1 Shahadah – the declaration of faith
2 Salah – offering five prayers a day
3 Zakah – giving 2.5 per cent of one's wealth to the poor
4 Sawm – fasting, including in the month of Ramadan
5 Hajj – pilgrimage to Makkah (Mecca) in Saudi Arabia.

The Five Pillars are based on the Qur'an and Hadith.

Shi'a Muslims base their faith on the Ten Obligatory Acts. These acts include four of these pillars, with the addition of:

+ Khums – tax set at 20 per cent of one's savings for causes determined by Shi'a leaders
+ Jihad – striving in the way of Allah
+ Amr bil-Ma`ruf – enjoining good
+ Nahy `anil-Munkar – forbidding evil
+ Tawalla – love and devotion (particularly towards the ahl al-bayt)
+ Tabarra – disassociation (from opponents of the ahl al-bayt).

Five Pillars (Sunni)   **Ten Obligatory Acts (Shi'a)**

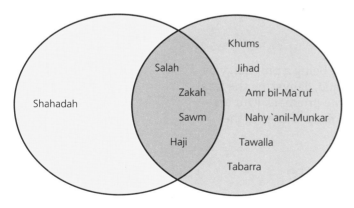

These divinely mandated practices are often performed at specific times and places. Muslims believe that there is a close relationship between the outward actions and intention behind them. The purpose is not mere rote repetition but to demonstrate faith and obedience to Allah. This was taught by the Prophet Muhammad: 'The reward of deeds depends upon the intentions and every person will get the reward according to what he has intended.' (Hadith – Bukhari).

This reminds Muslims that Allah knows their hearts and thoughts. It also reassures people who are physically unable to carry out actions such as prayer and fasting that they will still benefit if they have the proper intentions.

Shahadah

Shahadah means testimony or witness. The Shahadah is the first pillar for Sunni Muslims and represents a declaration of faith. For Shi'a Muslims, Shahadah is a belief rather than a practice and therefore not included in the Ten Obligatory Acts. However, it is represented in three of the five roots of Usul al-Din, namely tawhid, nubuwwah and Imamate (see Chapter 4) and so is still part of their beliefs.

The Shahadah contains two fundamental statements:

> 'I bear witness that there is no god except Allah; He is one and has no partner.
>
> And I bear witness that Muhammad is His Servant and Messenger.'

Many Shi'a Muslims add to the Shahadah:

> 'And I bear witness that Ali is the Friend of God.'

This is because of their belief in Ali as the rightful leader after Muhammad.

The first part of the Shahadah relates to tawhid, the second to risalah and nubuwwah (two of the six articles of faith and Usul al-Din). For Shi'a Muslims, the third statement also links to Imamah (one of the Usul al-Din).

Risalah 'Message', referring to belief in Prophets/Messengers of Allah

Shahadah as recognition of tawhid

REVISED

Muslims believe that Allah commanded Muhammad to preach strict monotheism (tawhid), in opposition to the polytheism of the Jahiliyya (see Chapter 1). Polytheism is the worship of multiple gods and classified as idolatry. In Islam, idolatry is shirk (setting up partners or equals with Allah), the worst sin and the only one that has been described as unforgivable (if believers do not repent during their lifetime). Because the Shahadah is an expression of tawhid, it is an important cornerstone of Muslim faith.

Muslims believe that Allah is all-forgiving. While the Qur'an states that Allah will not forgive shirk (Qur'an 4: 48), many Muslims believe that this refers only to this life. Elsewhere, the Qur'an states, 'My servants who have harmed yourselves by your own excess, do not despair of God's mercy. God forgives all sins: He is truly the Most Forgiving, the Most Merciful.' (Qur'an 39: 53). Therefore, if a person repents before dying, Allah can forgive their sin.

It is an important Muslim belief that Muhammad, while being a prophet, was still only a man. As a messenger, Muhammad was unique, delivering the final and universal message to the world. He is 'the seal of the prophets' (Qur'an 33: 40) and the greatest inspiration for Muslims who look up to him as the exemplary Muslim leader.

Shahadah as both public and private declaration of faith

REVISED

The Shahadah is the basis for all actions of a Muslim, including the Five Pillars and six articles of faith. It is seen both as a matter of personal faith and a public declaration.

Personal faith	Public declaration	
The Shahadah: + confirms a Muslim's recognition and acceptance of the oneness of Allah and the prophethood of Muhammad + puts Allah first in all aspects of life + is repeated in private prayer + marks important occasions, such as birth and death	The Shahadah: + is recited during the call to prayer and Salah + is repeated when someone wishes to convert to Islam, with a witness such as an imam present + is a reminder for Muslims to bear witness to the truth of Islam by sharing it with others	

Some Muslims consider the Shahadah to be more important as an expression of personal belief because every person will be accountable for themselves before God. Others say that the public declaration of the Shahadah helps to unite and strengthen the ummah, as well as to spread the message of Islam. Either way, the Shahadah is a practical way for a Muslim to bear witness to their faith.

Now test yourself   TESTED ◯

1 What are the two parts of the Sunni Shahadah?
2 What is the additional part recited by Shi'a Muslims?
3 State three occasions when the Shahadah is recited by Muslims.
4 Identify two purposes of the ummah.

Salah, worship and other forms of prayer

Salah

REVISED ◯

Muslims believe that the purpose of every person's life is to worship Allah (Qur'an 51: 56). There are many ways in which a Muslim can fulfil this obligation, but the highest form is the formal prayers known as Salah. Salah is one of the Sunni Five Pillars and Shi'a Ten Obligatory Acts and is regarded as a way of establishing a direct and lasting relationship with Allah, attaining taqwa (God-consciousness), receiving comfort and keeping away from sin.

> **Salah** Five daily prayers
>
> **Wudu** Ritual washing before Salah

The Hadith state that the first question a Muslim will be asked on the Day of Judgement is about Salah. This makes Muslims very conscious of fulfilling this duty, particularly those for whom it is compulsory: men, women (except under some conditions, including those who are menstruating or have just given birth) and children from around the age of ten.

Wudu (ablution)

Salah is both a physical and spiritual act and must begin with a washing ritual known as wudu (ablution). The minor ablution consists of a sequence of washing or wiping various parts of the body with water, including the head and feet. Not only does this ensure physical cleanliness, but also reminds a worshipper to approach prayer with a pure mind and heart. Salah without wudu is not valid. The major ablution (ghusl) is required when the entire body needs to be clean, such as after sex or menstruation. Care must be taken with personal appearance and appropriate clothing, as Salah is seen as a meeting with Allah.

> 'If there was a river at the door of anyone of you and he took a bath in it five times a day would you notice any dirt on him?' They said, 'Not a trace of dirt would be left.' The Prophet added, 'That is the example of the five prayers with which Allah blots out (annuls) evil deeds.'

(Hadith – Bukhari)

Times for Salah

The Qur'an (4: 103) instructs Muslims to offer Salah at set times during the day with a prescribed number of rak'ahs (cycles) in each.

There are five daily prayers:
+ Salah al-Fajr – before sunrise
+ Salah al-Zuhr – noon
+ Salah al-Asr – late afternoon
+ Salah al-Maghrib – just after sunset
+ Salah al-Isha – later in the evening.

Prayers are spread out over the course of the day to bring the Muslim's mind back to their purpose – to worship Allah – and to put this duty above all others.

Each Salah is preceded by the adhan (call to prayer), called by a muezzin, announcing the time of the prayer.

While Muslims will try to observe each Salah on time, work and other commitments can sometimes make this challenging. In some circumstances, some prayers, like Salah al-Zuhr and Salah al-Asr, can be combined. Additionally, the cycles in some of the prayers must be halved if a person is travelling a distance.

> **Adhan** The call to prayer
>
> **Muezzin** Muslim who makes the call to prayer

Direction

> Turn your face in the direction of the Sacred Mosque: wherever you [believers] may be, turn your faces to it.

(Qur'an 2: 144, Haleem 2008)

The direction of prayer during Salah is known as qiblah. Muslims must face Makkah, which is where the Ka`bah is located. This is for the sake of unity – it is not because the Ka`bah is being worshipped. The exception to the rule of qiblah is when someone is travelling in a vehicle or is immobile due to health reasons.

Recitations

Salah must be offered in Arabic and from memory using set prayers taken from the Qur'an, Sunnah and Hadith. One example recitation is Allahu Akbar, which means 'God is the greatest'. This is one way that the Qur'an and Muhammad are commemorated daily by Muslims, although the focus is always on Allah. The sajdah position allows for Muslims to offer prayers for a specific purpose in their own language and words in the additional optional prayers.

There are some varying practices in Shi'a Islam:
+ Salah al-Zuhr and Salah al-Asr are offered together (four + four cycles), as are Salah al-Maghrib and Salah al-Isha (three + four cycles). This is because Muhammad occasionally did the same (Hadith – Bukhari 543) which Shi'a Muslims say was to make offering the prayers more practical in their daily life.
+ They put a clay or earthen tablet called turba on the ground where they will place their head in prostration. This is because Muhammad and early Muslims used to prostrate directly on the earth or something natural (Hadith – Bukhari 836), rather than on carpets. This is a reminder that everyone has come from the earth and will return to it. The turba should preferably be from Karbala, Iraq, due to its sacred status for Shi'a Muslims (see Festivals and commemorations, page 62).

Concentration

For some Muslims, the preparation, process and performance of prayer may appear very ritualistic and some may find it difficult to concentrate, particularly when they are busy, lack motivation or are facing difficulties. Proper Salah, however, must start with niyyah (intention), to focus the mind on the prayer to be offered. Muslims believe Salah should be offered with complete attentiveness and a desire to connect with Allah and not solely as a ritualistic act of piety. Any distractions could make Salah void and the Qur'an condemns those who are not mindful during their prayers (Qur'an 107: 4–5), as this will be of no benefit to them.

> When Jibril (Gabriel) appeared to the Prophet as a man and asked 'What is Ihsan (perfection)?' Allah's Apostle replied, 'To worship Allah as if you see Him, and if you cannot achieve this state of devotion then you must consider that He is looking at you.'

(Hadith – Bukhari)

Niyyah Intention

Salah at home

Men should, as far as possible, offer Salah in a mosque. Women are excused from Salah during menstruation. As an alternative, including for men for whom going to a mosque may be difficult, Salah can be offered at home, work or other suitable places. The Prophet Muhammad taught Muslims not to leave their homes empty of spirituality:

> Pray in your houses – do not make them like graveyards.

(Hadith – Bukhari)

In some extreme circumstances, prayer is advised only in homes. In the early days of Islam, torrential rain meant that prayers at the mosque were suspended. During the coronavirus pandemic some Muslim countries instructed people to pray at home based on this precedent. Muslim leaders in the UK also did the same.

Families ensure that a clean area of the house, with as few distractions as possible, is designated for Salah. Salah at home is usually led by the head of the household. A compass or mobile phone app can be used to determine the qiblah.

Now test yourself

5 Identify two similarities and two differences in the way Sunni and Shi'a Muslims offer Salah.

TESTED ◯

Other forms of prayers

REVISED ◯

In addition to Salah, there are optional forms of worship that Muslims are encouraged to offer.

+ The **nawafil** (extra prayers) – prayers that can be offered throughout the day outside Salah. These are rewarded by Allah, as a believer has gone out of their way to offer extra prayers.
+ **Tahajjud** (pre-dawn prayer) – a nafl prayer specifically offered late at night, before Salah al-Fajr. It carries particular blessings as the worshipper has given up sleep for the sake of Allah. The Prophet used to offer night prayers until his feet became swollen. Aishah asked him, 'Why do you do this when Allah has forgiven your previous and future faults?' He replied, 'Shouldn't I be a thankful servant (of Allah)?' (Hadith – Bukhari)
+ **Du'a** (supplication) – literally means 'cry (of the heart)' or to summon. This is usually performed with the raising of hands. Set prayers are recited and the person prays for anything they wish. This can be offered individually or collectively.
+ **Tasbih** – means 'glorifying' (Allah) and, like du'a, is not a formal prayer. Many Muslims use tasbih beads to remind them of the names of Allah. Du'a and tasbih can be offered at any time, including instinctively.
+ **Wird** – a devotional form of prayer, including recitation of the Qur'an, found in Sufi orders with the purpose of achieving nearness to Allah. This can extend to hymns and dancing too, as performed by the Whirling Dervishes of the Turkish Mevlevi order (see Chapter 6).

Jummah prayer

The most important part of the week is the offering of the Jummah prayer on Friday afternoon. Muslims congregate in mosques to listen to a sermon (khutbah) by the imam and worship together. Muslims are told in the Qur'an to 'leave off your trading' and 'hurry towards the reminder of God' on this day (Qur'an 62: 9–10). This highlights Jummah as an important prayer for the purposes of unity and harmony in the ummah. There is no day of rest in Islam so Muslims are free to return to work after the Jummah prayer.

The Jummah prayer replaces the Salat al-Zuhr, but is shortened from four cycles to two cycles as the sermon counts as part of the prayer and therefore must be listened to in silence. There are many blessings linked to Jummah as it is an opportunity for sins to be forgiven, and as a congregational prayer, it promotes community and provides opportunities for believers to reconnect and ensure each other's well-being.

Qur'an 62: 9 is generally interpreted as meaning that attendance at the Jummah prayer is compulsory; Muhammad said that a person who misses three consecutive Jummah prayers, without a proper excuse, suffers a loss of faith. This indicates the great significance of Jummah as a prayer for the ummah. However, as it is not part of the Five Pillars of Islam, it is not considered more important than the five daily prayers. Furthermore, many Muslims may struggle to attend the Jummah prayer every week due to work or other commitments, but still offer the main prayers as it is these – not Jummah – that they will be questioned about on the Day of Judgement.

Shi'a Muslims do not believe the Jummah prayer is necessary in the absence of the twelfth Imam (see Chapter 4: Imamate), though many still perform it.

Research activity

Why do Shi'a Muslims not think it is necessary to offer Jummah in the absence of the twelfth imam?

Now test yourself

6 Give three ways that the Jummah prayer is important for the ummah.

7 Summarise the importance of the Jummah prayer in no more than 30 words.

TESTED

The mosque (masjid)

The mosque is the beating heart and spiritual home of the Muslim community. Muhammad's first action on arrival in Madinah was to build a mosque. This mosque, known as Al-Masjid al-Nabawi, became the religious, political, educational and social headquarters for the city and helped to establish the concept of the ummah (community of Muslims) which continues to this day. Therefore, the mosque is the hub of the ummah, playing a pivotal role in making Muslims feel like they belong to a global family made up of brothers and sisters in faith and promoting a spirit of unity.

The ummah

Community life is central in Islam. It is linked to belief in tawhid – just as Allah is one, so should humanity be one. Muslims are encouraged to support and help each other, both in good and challenging times, to prevent anyone from feeling lonely and isolated. Historically, Muslims have marked important social occasions together, like births and weddings. They also come together for religious purposes such as prayers, Jummah, festivals and Hajj as a symbol of unity between people regardless of gender, age, race or status, all submitting themselves completely to Allah.

Nowadays, Muslims live in very diverse societies in the West. The concept of ummah helps them to keep an Islamic way of life and to stay strong in their faith, particularly if they feel they are threatened at a time of increased Islamophobia.

The Arabic word for mosque is 'masjid', literally 'a place of prostration', which signifies its most important primary function: prayer. All of the five daily prayers are offered in mosques, led by an imam, and Muslims are told to attend (Qur'an 9: 18). Worshippers must keep straight rows and stand shoulder to shoulder. This symbolises unity, equality and brotherhood/sisterhood. Men and women traditionally pray in separate areas.

Exam tip

Do not confuse imams (with a lower case i) with the infallible Imams (with a capital I) in the Shi'a tradition.

Prayer with the congregation is 27 times better than prayer performed by oneself.

(Hadith – Bukhari)

The (whole) earth has been made a mosque and a means of purification for me, so wherever a person of my ummah may be when the time for prayer comes, let them pray.

(Hadith – Sahih Bukhari, 335)

These Hadiths may appear to be contradictory, however Muslims believe they are not, as they indicate:
✚ Allah has made the world spacious enough for people to worship Him anywhere
✚ prayer is more blessed when offered with others.

A mosque is used for other religious purposes including:
✚ celebrating key festivals such as Id-ul-Fitr and Id-ul-Adha
✚ marking important rites of passage and providing support to families for occasions such as an aqiqah (ceremony marking the birth of a baby), khitan (circumcision), nikah (marriage contract) and funerals
✚ offering counselling to individuals and families, such as those requiring resolutions to disputes.

The changing role of the masjid

REVISED ⬤

In the time of Muhammad, the Al-Masjid al-Nabawi was a very simple structure, yet it served many purposes, primarily as a place of prayer but also as a centre for learning, governing and medical treatment, as well as being the military headquarters and a refuge for the poor and for travellers.

Some of the ways the Prophet's mosque was used are not relevant today (for example, as an army base and keeping prisoners of war), so the role of the mosque has developed over time. Above all, the masjid exists to serve the needs of the ummah, which are not static or the same everywhere.

Purpose	Type	Introduced	Practised today?
Celebrating key festivals such as Id-ul-Fitr and Id-ul-Adha (Sunni and Shi'a)	Religious	By Muhammad	Yes
Religious classes for children (madrasahs), study circles and lectures (Sunni and Shi'a)	Religious, educational	Contemporary	Yes
Military base and rehabilitation for prisoners of war	Socio-political	By Muhammad	No
Congregation halls (Husayniyahs) to hold mourning ceremonies for Imam Hussain during Muharram (Shi'a only)	Religious	Historical	Yes
Daily prayers and Jummah	Religious	By Muhammad	Yes
Politics, government and legal court	Socio-political and legal	By Muhammad	No, except where family matters are discussed and resolved according to shari'a principles
Spiritual leadership	Religious	By Muhammad	Yes, though imams are mostly leaders of their local communities rather than of the whole ummah
Libraries and bookshops	Social/educational	Contemporary	Yes
Engaging with politicians, other faith groups and the media	Social/political	Contemporary	Yes
Hosting open days and school visits	Social/educational	Contemporary	Yes

A believer in a mosque is like a fish in water.

(A saying attributed to Malik ibn Dinar, a Persian scholar and traveller)

Charitable giving

Support for the poor is a key part of Islam. Muslims believe that giving and spending in the way of Allah, and the difference this makes to others, strengthens the ummah. This liberationist philosophy (an emphasis on social equality and the circulation of wealth to serve the needy) helps to make sure that no member of the community is neglected and is one of the ways that society can be at peace – one of the meanings and aims of Islam.

Zakah

> *None of you [believers] will attain true piety unless you give out of what you cherish: whatever you give, God knows about it very well.*

(Qur'an 3: 92, Haleem 2008)

Zakah, also called almsgiving, is the third of the Sunni Five Pillars and fourth of the Shi'a Ten Obligatory Acts. Making a financial sacrifice is a way for believers to attain nearness to Allah. While many beliefs and practices are shared, there are also differences between Sunni and Shi'a Muslims in relation to Zakah:

Sunni	Shi'a
All Muslims consider Zakah, the giving of a proportion of one's wealth to help the poor, as an essential obligation for all who own 'nisab' (a minimum threshold of wealth based on the price of a specific amount of gold)	
Sunni Muslims use qiyas (reasoning) (Chapter 3) to decide how much to donate – about 2.5% of their total wealth in all forms. This is to prevent wealth becoming 'idle' and not being used for any social benefit	Shi'a Muslims calculate Zakah based on how much of specific commodities they own: coinage, cattle and crops. Nowadays, many Shi'a Muslims don't own these things and are not strictly obliged to donate Zakah at all. It is instead 'mustahab' (recommended)
In Muslim countries, Zakah is collected directly by the state. In the UK, it is made as a confidential donation to the local mosque/masjid	
Muslims are also encouraged to provide voluntary aid to their communities in the form of money or good deeds, called sadaqah, and, in the UK, to registered charities	
	Though Shi'a Muslims may not pay Zakah, they do pay Khums which is one-fifth (khums) of their savings, after they have deducted their living expenses, for the benefit of other causes too

Passages in the Qur'an, such as Qur'an 9: 60, specify the things Zakah can be used for, including:

+ relieving poverty
+ helping those in debt
+ providing assistance for travellers
+ paying ransom for prisoners of war
+ improving the welfare of society in any other way.

The Qur'an states that those in need of Zakah can often be identified by characteristics such as their appearance, and that just because they do not ask for help does not mean they do not need it: 'you will recognize them by their characteristic of not begging persistently' (Qur'an 2: 273).

All acts of charity, including Zakah, are compared to a loan which will be repaid by Allah: 'Keep up the prayer, pay the prescribed alms, and lend God a good loan' (Qur'an 73: 20).

Those who pay Zakah and make personal financial sacrifices are also counted among the successful believers (Qur'an 23: 4).

Sadaqah

REVISED ●

While Zakah is complulsory for Sunni Muslims who own the nisab threshold and is set at a fixed amount, there are other types of charity in Islam which are optional and can be of any amount. One of these is sadaqah. Sadaqah is not just financial and can also extend to deeds, such as kindness to animals, planting a tree and offering a smile.

Every kindly act is considered charity.

(Hadith)

There is also sadaqah jariyah (ongoing charity) which is an act which continues to benefit others after a person's death.

Khums

REVISED ●

In the time of Muhammad, Khums primarily applied to the spoils of war. Following his death, Shi'a Muslims interpreted this verse to apply to their Imams and since then they have given 20 per cent of their annual savings to the Imam of the time to spend it on whatever he thinks necessary for the community. In the absence of the twelfth and final Imam (see Chapter 6), Khums is paid to one of his representatives called the Marja' Taqlid (source of emulation) – also known as the Grand Ayatollah – who decides how the money should be used. This usually goes towards the building of mosques, schools, orphanages and other religious causes.

Like Zakah, Khums must be paid annually. Shi'a Muslims believe that failure to do so is a violation of the Prophet Muhammad or the Imams' right to the funds. Nizari Shi'a Muslims give approximately 10 per cent of their monthly income as both Zakah and Khums.

The commitment of Muslims to give Zakah, Khums and sadaqah means that they are one of the groups who donate most to charities in the UK. This spirit of giving has an enormous impact on the ummah too, ensuring that people's needs are met and the community is united.

> **Revision activity**
>
> Create a Venn diagram with two overlapping circles, one for Zakah and the other for Khums, and write down the similarities and differences between them.

Hajj

Hajj is a pilgrimage to Makkah in Saudi Arabia. Makkah is the holiest city on Earth for Muslims, as it is where prophets like Ibrahim, Isma'il and Muhammad lived and preached.

Making a pilgrimage to Makkah is obligatory for all Muslims who are physically able and can afford it (Qur'an 3: 97). Muslims are not expected to attempt Hajj if there is no safe route to Makkah. Hajj must be completed at least once in a Muslim's life, and someone who has completed Hajj is given the honorific title 'Hajji' (for men) or 'Hajjah' (for women).

Origins of Hajj

REVISED ●

The origins of pilgrimage can be traced back around 4,000 years to the time of Ibrahim. According to the Qur'an (2: 125), Ibrahim and his son Isma'il were commanded by Allah to rebuild the Ka'bah, and this restored the city as a place of pilgrimage.

> The Ka'bah (cube-shaped building in Makkah) is believed to be more than 5,000 years old, and the first masjid (mosque) in the world dedicated to the worship of one God. This makes it the holiest site in Islam and the focus of the Hajj. The Ka'bah has also been called other names in the Qur'an, such as Bayt al-Atiq (ancient house) and Bayt al-Haram (sacred house).

Muslims have been travelling to Makkah to complete the Hajj ever since the time of Muhammad. In recent years, the nature of the pilgrimage has changed with the worldwide spread of Islam and the introduction of fast, direct travel by plane, car and train, which has made access to Makkah much easier. As a result, Hajj has become one of the largest annual gatherings of people anywhere in the world, with approximately 3 million pilgrims making the journey every year. Hajj is seen to be a powerful demonstration of the unity of the ummah, with Muslims from different denominations and countries converging in one place for the purpose of worshipping Allah and fulfilling a requirement of their faith.

> Proclaim the Pilgrimage to all people. They will come to you on foot and on every kind of lean camel, emerging from every deep mountain pass to attain benefits and mention God's name, on specified days, over the livestock He has provided for them. Feed yourselves and the desperately poor from them. Then let the pilgrims perform their acts of cleansing, fulfil their vows, and circle around the Ancient House.

(Qur'an 22: 27–9, Haleem 2008)

The timing of Hajj is based on the lunar calendar, culminating with the festival of Id-ul-Adha. This is two months and ten days after Id-ul Fitr. The pilgrimage starts on the eighth day of the last month of the Islamic calendar, Dhu al-Hijjah, and lasts about five days.

Performance of Hajj

Prepare to enter Makkah	• Men wear two unsewn pieces of white cloth (ihram). Unlike Sunni Muslims, Shi'a Muslims also cover their shoulders. • Women dress in simple clothes of one colour, usually white. Women must be accompanied by a mahram (a male relative with whom marriage is not permissible, or their husband). • Ihram symbolises that all believers are equal before Allah. • Ihram also represents an attitude, reminding Muslims to keep their minds pure of any grudges, worries and desires. • Ihram cloths are used by some people as shrouds when they die, reinforcing that this life is a preparation for the next. • Pilgrims make niyyah (intention) when they put on their ihram.
Perform tawaf	• Tawaf is making seven anti-clockwise circuits of the Ka`bah, starting from the hajri aswad (a black stone or meteorite Muslims believe was sent by Allah). • If possible, pilgrims kiss the hajri aswad.
Perform sa`ee	• The sa`ee is a brisk walk or run between two hills, Safa and Marwa, completed seven times. • It re-enacts Hajar's (Ibrahim's wife) search for help when she and Isma'il were thirsty in the desert. When Isma'il's heels struck the ground a fountain miraculously sprouted in the shape of a blessed well. This well is known as Zamzam and pilgrims drink water from it.
Pray at Mina	• Pilgrims spend a day and night at Mina, four miles east of Makkah, offering all five Salah.
Perform wuquf	• Wuquf means 'standing'. • Pilgrims pray for forgiveness on the plain of Arafat, nine miles from Makkah. They stay in tents during wuquf. • This stage is often described as the climax of Hajj, as the practice of wuquf symbolises what will happen on the Day of Judgement when everyone must stand in front of Allah.
Stone the Anti-Christ	• Pilgrims collect pebbles at Muzdalifah for the ramy al-jimar (stoning of walls representing evil). They sleep under the sky at night. • This is to re-enact Ibrahim driving away the Anti-Christ when it tried to tempt him to disobey Allah.
Have an animal sacrificed	• At the end of Hajj, pilgrims who can afford it arrange to have an animal sacrificed. The meat is distributed to people who need it.
Trim hair and remove ihram	• Men shave their heads, symbolising new life and forgiveness of past sins. Women cut only a lock of their hair. All pilgrims return to normal dress.
Return to Ka`bah for tawaf and sa`ee	• Pilgrims perform a farewell tawaf and repeat the run between Safa and Marwa.

➕ Shi'a Muslims perform an additional tawaf in order to resume sexual relations with their spouses. They visit the tombs of members of the ahl al-bayt – part of the wider Shi'a practice of Ziyara (visitation) that includes pilgrimage at some point in their lives to the graves of their Imams including Imam Ali, whose grave they believe to be in Najaf, Iraq (considered by Shi'as to be the holiest site after Makkah and Madinah), and Imam Hussain in Karbala, Iraq.

A-level Religious Studies: Islam

+ Nizari Isma'ili Muslims make a pilgrimage to the living Imam, a ritual known as Hajj-i-Batini. This is based on the Qur'an's teaching about people visiting Ibrahim (Qur'an 22: 27) to become closer to Allah.

Throughout the rites of Hajj, pilgrims are expected to maintain a state of continuous worship and repentance. Muhammad stated that a person who completes the Hajj emerges as sinless as a newborn child.

While the Hajj must take place in a specific month, Muslims can make a smaller pilgrimage at other times of the year. This is known as umrah and involves less time and fewer rituals.

Although the primary purpose of Hajj is to fulfil an individual duty to obey Allah's will, it is also an opportunity to engage in trade (Qur'an 2: 198). This is allowed so that believers are not denied opportunities to discuss or do business when there are so many people gathered together. Because of this, for some people, the pilgrimage is more than just a personal journey of religious enquiry and shows Islam as a practical faith.

> **Revision activity**
>
> Create a memorable image for each stage of the Hajj, then practise rewriting the information from memory.

> **Now test yourself**   TESTED ◯
>
> 8 Write down three aims of Hajj.

Sawm and Ramadan

Sawm

REVISED ◯

Sawm is the Arabic word for fasting. Sawm is one of the Five Pillars in Sunni Islam and one of the Ten Obligatory Acts for Shi'a Muslims. There are two types of fasting in Islam:

1 optional – weekly, following the practice of the Prophet Muhammad
2 compulsory – during the month of Ramadan.

> **Sawm** Fasting

For Muslims, fasting involves giving up food and drink, sex, and close intimacy such as kissing. Additionally, there is the fasting of the eyes, ears, tongue, hands and feet, meaning they are not to be used for any disobedience of Allah's commands.

Fasting starts at the first light of dawn and ends at sunset. The Prophet Muhammad would eat something at the start of the fast (suhur) and break the fast at the end (iftar) with dates and water, and Muslims follow his example. The quantity of food consumed at suhur and iftar should be moderate – people are discouraged from eating too much.

Muslims believe that there are many religious and moral benefits to fasting:

+ It helps them to get close to Allah and develop spirituality and taqwa.
+ The extra prayers offered, especially at night, receive special acceptance from Allah.
+ Hunger and thirst help them to appreciate the suffering of the less fortunate.
+ Fasting instils self-restraint and gives Muslims an opportunity to reflect on what they say and do, how they behave and treat others, and to try to reform accordingly. Reminding themselves of their own faults encourages them to make allowances for the weaknesses of others.

They believe that there are health benefits as well as spiritual ones. Therefore, Muslims generally see fasting as a blessing rather than a burden. The Prophet Muhammad said that whoever observed six fasts in Shawwal (the month that follows Ramadan) would derive the equivalent of blessings of fasting for the entire year.

Only people who are physically able to fast are required to do so. People who are exempt from fasting include:

+ the sick
+ travellers on long journeys (for example, flying abroad)
+ elderly people whose health would be affected
+ people taking medication that requires food
+ menstruating, pregnant and breastfeeding women
+ young children (the age of fasting varies in different Muslim communities).

According to the Qur'an, the reason for excusing these people from fasting is because Allah recognises their situation and 'wants ease for you, not hardship' (Qur'an 2: 185). However, some of these groups will have to make up for the missed fasts at a later date.

Ramadan

Ramadan is the month when the angel Jibril first visited Muhammad to reveal the Qur'an (see Chapter 2). Ramadan lasts either 29 or 30 days, starting with the sighting of the crescent moon and ending with the festival of Id-ul-Fitr. The lunar calendar is not fixed, so the length of each daily fast depends on the time of year Ramadan falls in and where in the world it is being observed.

All Muslims who are in good health (except for those who are exempt – see above) are required to fast during Ramadan. Apart from children and the elderly, Muslims who cannot keep the fast in Ramadan must either make up the missed days at another time, or pay fidya, a monetary donation that supports the poor. While fasting, Muslims spend their time reflecting on Allah's blessings and attributes as a means of avoiding inappropriate thoughts and actions. Muhammad made it clear that the purpose of observing Ramadan was self-improvement and condemned people who neglect this while observing the fast. He said that Allah would rather people mended their behaviour than perform the fast: 'Whoever does not give up lying and evil deeds and saying bad words to others then God is not in need of their leaving food and drink.' (Hadith – Bukhari).

There are some particular differences in the way that Shi'a Muslims observe Ramadan:

+ The fast is broken a little later than sunset, when darkness has set in: 'until the white thread of dawn becomes distinct from the black' (Qur'an 2: 187).
+ The martyrdom of the first Imam, Ali, is also commemorated during the month, on the days he was attacked (19th) and died (21st).

Commemorating the Night of Power (Laylat al-Qadr)

Ramadan was the month when Muhammad received the first of many Qur'anic revelations, an event known as the Night of Power (Laylat al-Qadr) (see Chapter 2).

This means that there is a special link between the Qur'an and the month of Ramadan and Muslims spend the month reciting the Qur'an more frequently. They try to recite the whole Qur'an within Ramadan, as the angel Jibril did with the Prophet. One way many Sunni Muslims achieve this through a voluntary prayer known as tarawih, offered after Salat al-Isha, a tradition that started in the time of the second Caliph, Umar. Shi'a Muslims do not offer the tarawih prayer, as it was not the Prophet's practice.

> **Tarawih** Additional night prayers in Ramadan (Sunni)

Muslims also strive to experience their own Laylat al-Qadr. This is a night when a person has all their prayers accepted, or a moment when angels come to support them. When this happens, it is 'better than a thousand months' (Qur'an 97: 3), which means that no one can measure the extent of its impact and rewards.

61

For Sunni Muslims, this is done in the last ten days of Ramadan, particularly during the odd-numbered nights. Shi'a Muslims seek the Night of Power on the 19th, 21st and 23rd nights of Ramadan. For this reason, mosques are very busy in the last ten days of Ramadan. Some Muslims spend this time in i'tikaf (retreat), during which they have a private space in the mosque to study, worship and rest.

Muslims believe that the Night of Power can remove past sins: 'Whoever spends this night in prayer out of faith and in the hope of reward will be forgiven their previous sins' (Hadith).

The end of Ramadan is marked by the joyous festival of Id-ul-Fitr.

Now test yourself TESTED ⬤

9   Summarise the importance of the Night of Power for:
   a) Prophet Muhammad (maximum 40 words) (refer back to chapter 2)
   b) all Muslims (maximum 40 words).
   Include the words: Jibril, Qur'an, Ramadan, prayers, retreat.

Festivals and commemorations

All Muslims celebrate two main festivals – Id-ul-Adha and Id-ul-Fitr – while Shi'a Muslims have two additional commemorations, Id al-Ghadir and Ashura.

Id-ul-Adha   REVISED ⬤

History

Id-ul-Adha means the festival of sacrifice. It takes place on the 10th day of the Islamic month of Dhu al-Hijjah and commemorates the story of Ibrahim and Isma'il's obedience to Allah (Qur'an 37: 102–7). Ibrahim had a dream that he was sacrificing Isma'il. He interpreted it to mean that Allah wanted him to sacrifice Isma'il (child sacrifice was a common cultural practice at this time). Isma'il was willing to be sacrificed as he believed Allah commanded it. When Ibrahim was about to sacrifice Isma'il, Allah called out to him to stop. Even though the dream had been intended to symbolise something else, Allah praised both of them for their spirit of devotion. A ram was sacrificed instead.

How Id-ul-Adha is celebrated today

+ During the Hajj, in the desert of Mina, animals are sacrificed and their meat is shared out among people in need. This is called 'qurbani' (from the word 'qurb', connoting nearness and love between two people). It is also known as udhiyyah (sacrifice). Many Muslims in the UK arrange for this to be done in countries where halal (permissible) methods are used. 'Qurbani' is a reminder to Muslims that just as animals may be sacrificed for a higher purpose, so should they be prepared to give up their own lives for the sake of Allah.

+ People buy new clothes and families go to the mosque to offer a special Id salah prayer and listen to a sermon. Everyone says 'Id Mubarak' (Have a blessed Id) to each other. Id-ul-Adha is a public holiday in Muslim countries.

+ Id-ul-Adha is not merely a celebration of a story but a reminder to all Muslims to be ready to follow the example of Ibrahim and his family and offer themselves in Allah's service as taught in the Qur'an. It is this sacrifice that gave Ibrahim and his family the reward of being the ancestors of the Prophet Muhammad. Muslims are grateful for this and therefore offer prayers for them.

Id-ul-Fitr

Id-ul-Fitr takes place on the first day of Shawwal, the month following Ramadan. It is a joyous occasion when Muslims express their gratitude to Allah for the blessings of Ramadan. As on Id-ul-Adha, people wear new clothes, families go to the mosque to offer a special Id salah and listen to a sermon, and everyone says 'Id Mubarak' to each other. People exchange gifts and celebrate with food at home or in a restaurant. No fasting is allowed. The head of each family gives money known as 'zakat al-fitr' which goes towards less fortunate members of society. Id-ul-Fitr is also a public holiday in Muslim countries. Muslims emphasise that Id-ul-Fitr, while a social celebration, is first and foremost a religious occasion as it is supposed to remind Muslims to maintain the self-discipline and other benefits gained during Ramadan all year round.

Id al-Ghadir (Shi'a)

Muhammad received a revelation at a pond called Ghadir Khumm, instructing him to convey an important message (Qur'an 5: 67). He gathered the Muslims who were with him and announced: 'Whoever took me as his mawla (authority), Ali is his mawla.' (Hadith). Immediately afterwards, Muhammad received the last Qur'anic revelation, that Islam had been perfected for Muslims (Qur'an 5: 3). Shi'a Muslims believe that this means that Ali had been designated as Muhammad's successor. Id al-Ghadir is:

+ celebrated on the 18th of Dhul Hijjah (shortly after Hajj)
+ observed by Shi'a Muslims to mark the occasion when, they believe, Muhammad appointed Ali as the leader of Muslims after him
+ the most important of all Ids for Shi'a Muslims. It is celebrated in many ways, including eulogies of the ahl al-bayt, talks and entertainment. It is a public holiday in Iran and Iraq.

Ashura (Shi'a)

History

Ashura takes place on the 10th of Muharram and commemorates the anniversary of the martyrdom of Imam Hussain, the grandson of Muhammad and third Imam for Shi'a Muslims. He was martyred along with his family and companions in 680CE in Karbala, Iraq.

When Yazid became leader of the Muslims following the end of the Rightly Guided Caliphate, he demanded allegiance from Hussain. Hussain refused because Yazid was acting against the teachings of Islam and was ruling like a tyrant. While Hussain and 72 of his relatives and companions were heading towards Kufa in Iraq, Yazid sent an army to surround them in the desert of Karbala. Hussain refused to give Yazid their loyalty and were subsequently deprived of water and food. Yazid's army was under strict orders not to let Hussain and his people leave. Yazid's army martyred most of Hussain's party, including Hussain and his six-month-old son, and took the remaining women and children captive. Hussain's decapitated head was sent to the governor of Kufa.

How Ashura is commemorated today

+ Gatherings are held at the mosque every night from the first day of Muharram to Ashura. Mosques are usually draped in black and attendants also wear black to symbolise mourning.
+ Every year millions of Shi'a Muslims go on a pilgrimage to the shrine of Hussain in Karbala. The period of mourning stops 40 days after Ashura. This is because 40 days following the massacre, Hussain's family returned to Karbala to grieve over their loved ones.

+ Some Shi'a Muslims express their grief through poetry and ta'ziyah, a play to re-enact the death of Imam Hussain.
+ There is no fasting during Ashura.

The role of suffering

+ Some Shi'a Muslims carry out acts of self-flagellation as a symbol of their reverence and willingness to give their blood for the ahl al-bayt. By scratching and cutting themselves, they feel closer to Ali and Hussain who suffered greatly at the hands of their enemies. This is seen as an important expression of their devotion to the Imams.
+ Many Shi'a scholars reject such acts of self-harm which they see as excessive, arguing that they misrepresent Shi'a tradition, but consider more gentle methods, such as tapping oneself, acceptable. Some young Shi'a Muslims in Britain also choose to donate blood through the NHS to honour Hussain's sacrifice.
+ Critics of the practice of self-flagellation argue that Muhammad never led processions or struck himself for any purpose. Furthermore, there were many other martyrs in early Islam, but their deaths are not commemorated in the same manner. The Qur'an exhorts believers to be 'steadfast' at times of tragedy (Qur'an 2: 155–7) and the Prophet Muhammad also taught 'Wailing over the dead is one of the affairs of the days of Jahiliyya (ignorance)' (Hadith). Therefore, many question whether it is necessary to dwell on past injustices in this way.
+ Martyrs are praised highly in the Qur'an and becoming a martyr is one of the four noble ranks believers can attain (Qur'an 4: 69). Martyrs are also described as living in terms of their spirit and example (Qur'an 3: 169). This provides assurance to Muslims and reminds them to express grief in reaction to personal loss in a way that is permissible in the shari'a.

The massacre at Karbala and martyrdom of Hussain and other members of the ahl al-bayt is remembered by all Muslims, even though the rest of the ummah does not mark Ashura in the same way as Shi'a Muslims. Other Muslims still express love for Muhammad and his family and offer special prayers for them known as 'salawat ala al-Nabi'.

Ashura coincides with the anniversary of the time when Musa (Moses) and the Israelites were liberated from the Pharaoh in Egypt. On this day (and the day before and after), many Sunni Muslims fast, as this was the practice of Muhammad. Shi'a Muslims have been committed to maintaining the tradition of Ashura, seen largely through the pilgrimage of millions of people to Karbala, so that the sacrifices of past Imams and the ahl al-bayt are not forgotten and so Shi'a Muslims can also show similar courage in standing up to injustice.

> **Now test yourself** TESTED
>
> 10 Give a reason why Id al-Ghadir is the most important festival for Shi'a Muslims.

Revision activity

Write down arguments for and against marking Ashura through acts of self-flagellation.

Jihad

Jihad (meaning to struggle and strive) is one of the main duties of a Muslim. Sunni and Shi'a Muslims share belief in its importance. For Shi'a Muslims it is one of the Ten Obligatory Acts. The Prophet Muhammad said that Jihad is the pinnacle of faith (Hadith – Ibn Majah).

You who believe, be mindful of God, seek ways to come closer to Him and strive for His cause, so that you may prosper.

(Qur'an 5: 35, Haleem 2008)

Jihad Striving and struggling in the way of Allah

Suggested answer guidance to exam practice at **www.hoddereducation.co.uk/myrevisionnotesdownloads**

Based on the Hadith, there are two types of Jihad in Islam:

1 greater Jihad (al-Jihad al-akbar)
2 lesser Jihad (al-Jihad al-asghar).

A person who engages in Jihad is called a mujahid.

Greater Jihad

REVISED

The Qur'an says that the purpose of human creation is to worship Allah (Qur'an 51: 56). This goes deeper than just the performance of Salah but requires a Muslim to reflect Allah's attributes, such as love, mercy and kindness. This is not always easy, particularly as humans have been created weak (Qur'an 4: 28) and may easily succumb to temptation, which makes it difficult to live life in submission to Allah.

The role of greater Jihad is to struggle against evil and perform good deeds to become a better person. It is sometimes called 'inner Jihad'.

It is believed that through greater Jihad, a person can rise from the lowest state of being, known as nafs al-ammarah or self that is prone to evil (Qur'an 12: 53), to the highest level – nafs al-mutma'innah – the self at peace (Qur'an 89: 27), where the soul is purified and enjoys a lasting relationship with Allah. Muhammad said that the remembrance of Allah is better than gold, silver and fighting in the cause of Allah (Hadith – Ibne Majah).

Prayer, suppressing anger and helping the poor are all examples of greater Jihad and were also exemplified by Muhammad.

Lesser Jihad

REVISED

Lesser Jihad is the outward struggle to stop evil in the world mainly through physical or military methods, such as war.

Based on the Qur'an, Sunnah and Hadith, lesser Jihad is applicable – only as a last resort – when:

+ persecution threatens the life of believers
+ religious freedoms (such as the right to worship) are denied
+ Islamic countries have been attacked and need to be defended
+ a recognised Muslim leader (Prophet, Caliph or Imam) authorises it.

Additionally:

+ it is forbidden to target innocent civilians, including women, children and the elderly. Taking one innocent life is akin to killing all of humanity (Qur'an 5: 32)
+ the leaders of other faiths, trees and buildings cannot be attacked
+ violence must cease if there is an offer of peace (Qur'an 8: 61)
+ war must not be waged to gain converts: 'There is no compulsion in religion' (Qur'an 2: 256) and Muhammad's task was only to deliver the message of Islam (Qur'an 42: 48)
+ no mutilation is allowed as in the days of Jahiliyya
+ responses to attack must be proportionate (Qur'an 16: 126) and hatred from an enemy should be met with justice (Qur'an 5: 8)
+ prisoners should be treated with compassion
+ Muslims must fight not only for Islam but for people of all faiths, and are specifically commanded to protect buildings like synagogues and churches where 'God's name is much invoked' as well as the rights of people of other religions (Qur'an 22: 39–40).

Lesser Jihad in the time of Muhammad

Muhammad engaged in lesser Jihad during the persecution of early Muslims (see Chapter 2).

+ When Muhammad began preaching, he began to attract followers, including influential converts. The leaders of Makkah felt threatened by this and began to persecute Muslims.

+ During thirteen continuous years of persecution in Makkah, Muslims were taught never to retaliate or use violence. As Muslims lived in constant danger, the first set of migrants went to Abyssinia and the later ones to Yathrib (renamed Madinatul Nabi) to live in freedom and safety.
+ The Makkan oppressors came after the Muslims in Madinah and Muhammad received revelations from Allah instructing Muslims to defend themselves.

Fight in God's cause against those who fight you, but do not overstep the limits.

(Qur'an 2: 190, Haleem 2008)

Muslims say that this shows that Muhammad and his followers fought only as a last resort to defend their lives and freedom of belief. Muhammad opposed violence and sometimes forbade people from fighting when it clashed with other responsibilities, such as caring for their parents.

+ Despite being outnumbered and poorly equipped, 313 Muslims won the first battle at Badr against 1,000 Makkans. This success was repeated in further battles.
+ Larger battles, such as the Battle of Yarmouk in 636CE, led to victory for the Muslim army against a far larger Byzantine force.
+ Often Muslims would enter into peace agreements with various tribal groupings, including pagans and Jews with whom there was previously, or threat of, a war. However, their opponents did not always honour these agreements and would cause trouble and even attempted to infiltrate Islam with a view to destroying it from within. Muslims were permitted to retaliate against these conspiracies (Qur'an 9: 13).

Lesser Jihad today

Many Muslims argue that the context of the fighting in Muhammad's time is different from the modern world: there were no national laws and institutions like the United Nations which uphold human rights, including religious freedoms. They argue that while Muslims have basic rights where they live, such as freedom of conscience, there is no need for lesser Jihad – this is why some Muslims are pacifist.

On the other hand, some Muslims consider wars which are sanctioned by governments to be a modern example of lesser Jihad and consistent with Muhammad's reasons for engaging in war. In addition to obedience to Allah and Muhammad, Muslims are also commanded to obey 'those in authority among you' (Qur'an 4: 59) whether Muslim or not. For example, almost 6 million Muslims fought in the First and Second World Wars.

Misunderstandings about Jihad

REVISED

In recent years, terrorist groups like ISIS and Boko Haram have claimed to fight in the name of Islam. Their methods include kidnapping, torture and suicide bombings, with promises that martyrs in their cause will go to heaven. These actions mean that Jihad is viewed by some as offensive rather than defensive in nature.

The large majority of Muslims respond that terrorism has no justification in Islam. They point out that one of the meanings of Islam is 'peace'. Militant movements like ISIS have also targeted Muslims, even though the Qur'an forbids Muslims from killing each other (Qur'an 4: 93). The claim of the late ISIS leader Abu Bakr al-Baghdadi to be the Caliph for Muslims has also been largely rejected. Terrorist groups have been seen to grossly misrepresent the reasons and ways the Prophet Muhammad and the Rightly Guided Caliphs conducted lesser jihad.

Prominent Islamic scholars and organisations, from different sects and schools of thought around the world, have worked together to condemn all forms of extremism, radicalism and terrorism in the name of Islam.

Many Muslim organisations have attempted to address misconceptions about Jihad by organising regular peace symposiums and interfaith forums, actively encouraging fellow Muslims to donate blood and organising litter picking and tree planting initiatives. This is to highlight their commitment to peace, the environment and the well-being of everyone, whether Muslim or not.

Weapons of mass destruction

> Woe to every fault-finding backbiter who amasses riches, counting them over, thinking they will make him live for ever. No indeed! He will be thrust into the Crusher! What will explain to you what the Crusher is? It is God's Fire, made to blaze, which rises over people's hearts. It closes in on them in towering columns.

(Qur'an 104: 1–9, Haleem 2008)

The word 'Crusher' has been translated from the Arabic *hotamah* (similar sounding to 'atom'), which some Muslims say refers to a tiny particle storing immense energy that can destroy everything cast into it. Others say *hotamah* is a place. Some Muslims interpret these verses as referring to wealthy and powerful nations who would be responsible for creating fire, which would be extremely harmful to themselves as well as others.

> A flash of fire and smoke will be released upon you and no one will come to your aid.

(Qur'an 55: 35, Haleem 2008)

> Watch out for the Day when the sky brings forth clouds of smoke for all to see. It will envelop the people. They will cry, 'This is a terrible torment!'

(Qur'an 44: 10–11, Haleem 2008)

These teachings have been applied by modern interpretations to weapons of mass destruction (WMDs) to demonstrate the untold damage caused by their use. The impact of these weapons was demonstrated in 1945 when the United States of America dropped two atomic bombs on the Japanese cities of Hiroshima and Nagasaki. Nearly 200,000 people died and there were long-term physical and psychological effects, including later generations being born with severe genetic defects.

For this reason, the majority of Muslims oppose the use of WMDs as it runs counter to the principles and purpose of Islam, which is to protect life.

> If anyone kills a person – unless in retribution for murder or spreading corruption in the land – it is as if he kills all mankind, while if any saves a life it is as if he saves the lives of all mankind.

(Qur'an 5: 32, Haleem 2008)

Muslim leaders have also cautioned against the use of such weapons due to their devastating impact and have advised as well as prayed for heads of state to avoid their use.

Revision activity

How could you not fight a people who have broken their oaths, who tried to drive the Messenger out, who attacked you first? Do you fear them? It is God you should fear if you are true believers. Fight them: God will punish them at your hands, He will disgrace them, He will help you to conquer them, He will heal the believers' feelings.

(Qur'an 9: 13–14, Haleem 2008)

Read the passage above and:
+ highlight two or three parts and explain their importance
+ summarise the passage in your own words
+ match parts of the passage with the conditions for lesser Jihad.

Chapter summary

+ The Five Pillars (Sunni) and Ten Obligatory Acts (Shi'a) play a central role in fulfilling the purpose of the lives of Muslims to submit to the will of Allah and shaping and expressing their religious identity.
+ Festivals and commemorations hold an important place in the lives of Muslims as they serve as inspiring reminders of individuals and events that help to increase their faith and to bring the ummah together.
+ Jihad is another important belief and aims to bring about an improvement within oneself and society as a whole, primarily through spiritual means, as well as physical or military means if there is a danger to peace and human rights.

Exam practice

For OCR questions (AS and A-level exams) both AO1 knowledge and understanding and AO2 discussion and evaluation need to be included in an answer.
+ Think about making a point that presents one view in response to the question. Then explain that point using examples, key terms, quotes and maybe scholarly views.
+ Next, evaluate that view and show why it may have strengths and weaknesses, and explain and unpick these criticisms (how valid or successful are they). This is critical analysis.
+ Lastly, link back to the question.

To what extent is performing greater jihad more important than lesser jihad?
[OCR, AS, 30]

'Lesser jihad is still relevant today.' Discuss. [OCR, A-level, 40]

Consider the for and against arguments for this statement as they appear in the table opposite. Select any two points from either side, develop them into fuller points and formulate two paragraphs using the following structure in each:
+ argument (supporting the statement)
+ response (challenging the statement)
+ evaluation (reaching a judgement).

Suggested answer guidance to exam practice at **www.hoddereducation.co.uk/myrevisionnotesdownloads**

Refer to sources of authority and wisdom in your answer.

For	Against
+ Lesser Jihad is permitted in the Qur'an + It was the Sunnah of the Prophet Muhammad + Muslims have gone to war when conditions have been met (for example, nineteenth-century India, Bosnia in the 1990s) + Sunni and Shi'a Muslims believe that in the time of Isa (Jesus) and the Mahdi, war will be waged against non-believers	+ Islam is firmly established as a religion and no longer under threat + Lesser Jihad is not possible without a Caliph (Sunni) or Imam (Shi'a) + Modern warfare and machinery kill indiscriminately which contradict Muslim teachings about not harming the innocent + The Prophet said that there would be an end to religious wars in the time of Isa and the Mahdi

'Without the Shahadah, there is no Islam.' Evaluate this view.

[Eduqas, AO1 and AO2 25 (AS), 30 (A-level)]

Explore the diversity of Muslim practice of Salah. [Pearson Edexcel, AO1, 8]

6 Developments and diversity

This chapter covers the journey Islam took from unity at the time of Muhammad, to a diversity of belief and practice in the Muslim world today. This includes the origins of the Sunni and Shi'a split, approaches to understanding the Qur'an and the expression of faith found in the Sufi tradition.

Muslim unity during the lifetime of Muhammad

Islam lays great emphasis on unity.

> Hold fast to God's rope all together; do not split into factions.

(Qur'an 3: 103, Haleem 2008)

This is linked to strengthening belief in tawhid, serving Allah and his creation, which is the reason Prophets are sent (Qur'an 2: 213).

During the time of the Prophet, unity was straightforward – there was a single Muslim community. Muhammad was present to give guidance and all Muslims had given him bay'ah (pledge of allegiance) and agreed to obey him.

The early Sunni/Shi'a split

However, following the death of Muhammad, there were different opinions about who should lead the Muslim community, and this led to the split between Sunni and Shi'a Muslims.

+ **Muhajirun (from the Quraysh, the Prophet's tribe)**
  Abu Bakr, from the Quraysh, was chosen by community consensus (ijma') due to his piety and close friendship with Muhammad. Some 30,000 Muslims pledged allegiance to him. He became the first Rightly Guided Caliph. His followers became known as Sunni Muslims (from Ahl al-Sunnah or people of Muhammad's practice) and today they make up around 85 per cent of the ummah.
+ **Ahl al-bayt (the Prophet's family)**
  A minority of believers believed that authority should have gone to Ali, the Prophet's cousin and son-in-law, as he was from Muhammad's family. They do not recognise the authority of the first three Caliphs and consider Ali to be the first Imam. They became known as Shi'a Muslims (from Shi'at Ali, or party of Ali) and make up most of the rest of the ummah.

Suggested answer guidance to exam practice at **www.hoddereducation.co.uk/myrevisionnotesdownloads**

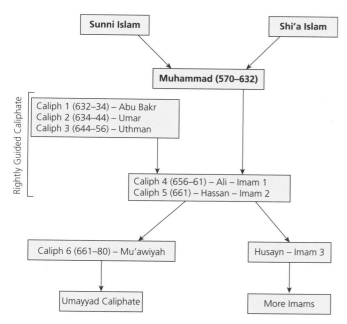

This shows how Sunni and Shi'a Muslims split after the death of Muhammad.

Hadith of the Pen and Paper

When Muhammad was dying, he wanted to write a statement to guide his followers after his death. Out of concern, Umar pointed out that the Prophet was seriously ill and that they had Allah's book (the Qur'an) with them, which was sufficient to guide them. Some agreed with Umar and didn't want to bother the dying Muhammad, while others wanted to give him pen and paper. Muhammad did not write anything in the end.

Shi'a Muslims believe that Muhammad intended to name his successor (in their eyes, Ali) and this was a ploy to divert attention away from this.

Now test yourself

TESTED

1 Why was unity easier in the time of the Prophet Muhammad?
2 What developments occurred after his death?
3 Give two reasons for the split after Muhammad's death.

Shi'a Muslims say that although Ali believed himself to be Muhammad's legitimate successor, he pledged loyalty to the first three Caliphs for the sake of maintaining unity. Sunni Muslims argue that the Qur'an instructs believers to be true to their promises (Qur'an 17: 34) and that Ali would have offered his allegiance to the first three Caliphs sincerely. He supported them fully and offered prayers behind them.

Sunni and Shi'a Muslims cite the following passages from the Qur'an and Hadith to support their position on leadership after Muhammad:

Sunni – Caliphate	Shi'a – Imamate
+ Allah promises Caliphate to those 'who believe and do good deeds' as a means of establishing Islam and tawhid, and providing them peace and security (Qur'an 24: 55) + 'If I were to take a Khalil (friend) other than my Lord, I would have taken Abu Bakr as such' (Hadith – Bukhari) + Abu Bakr accompanied Muhammad during the hijrah and was appointed to lead prayers during Muhammad's illness + 'Abu Bakr is the best among people except if a prophet is born' (Hadith) + Muhammad instructed that the Muslim leader should be from the Quraysh (Hadith – Musnad Ahmad)	+ The ahl al-bayt are free from sin: 'God wishes to keep uncleanness away from you, people of the [Prophet's] House, and to purify you thoroughly.' (Qur'an 33: 33) + Muhammad said: 'I leave you two weighty things. If you stick to both you will never go astray after me: the Book of Allah, and my progeny (Ahl al-Bayt)' (Hadith al-Thaqalayn) + Muhammad said, 'Whoever took me as his mawla (authority, guide), Ali is his mawla' (Hadith in Al-Ghadeer). After this, he received the final revelation of the Qur'an saying that Islam was complete (Qur'an 5: 3) + When Muhammad invited a Christian delegation to a mubahala (prayer challenge), he only brought the ahl al-bayt with him

You who believe, obey God and the Messenger, and those in authority among you. If you are in dispute over any matter, refer it to God and the Messenger, if you truly believe in God and the Last Day: that is better and fairer in the end.

(Qur'an 4: 59, Haleem 2008)

One who defected from obedience (to the leader) and separated from the main body of Muslims – if he dies in that state – would die the death of one belonging to the days of ignorance.

(Hadith – Muslim)

These teachings show the importance of following and obeying the right leader in Islam.

The Rightly Guided Caliphate

During the Rightly Guided Caliphate, there was extensive migration to other regions and considerable political, economic and social developments. Umar's caliphate divided the Islamic state into provinces and established an effective system of administration and governance. During Uthman's caliphate, Muslims defeated powerful empires and the faith spread to Tunisia, Central Asia, the Indian Ocean and Cyprus.

Their great and unlikely success, both for the protection and consolidation of the ummah, is evidenced from conflicts such as the Battle of Yarmouk when approximately 40,000 Muslims overcame an estimated 240,000-strong Byzantine army. Sunni Muslims say these achievements were through the efforts of the Rightly Guided Caliphs.

During this period, there were challenges to the authority of the Caliphs, including plots and conspiracies, and this caused considerable turmoil. Umar was attacked and both Uthman and Ali were assassinated by rebellious extremists. Ongoing disagreements about leadership meant that there was no longer unity among Muslims and in 661CE the Rightly Guided Caliphate came to an end. Sunni Muslims followed Mu'awiyah, who became the first caliph of the Umayyad dynasty, followed by his son Yazid, while others (Shi'a) pledged allegiance to the Imams from the ahl al-bayt.

Prophethood shall remain among you as long as Allah shall will. He will bring about its end and follow it with Caliphate on the precepts of prophethood for as long as He shall will and then bring about its end. A tyrannical monarchy will then follow and will remain as long as Allah shall will and then come to an end. There will follow thereafter monarchial despotism to last as long as Allah shall will and come to an end upon His decree. There will then emerge Caliphate on the precept of prophethood.

(Hadith – Musnad Ahmad)

Now test yourself TESTED ◯

4 Identify two successes and two challenges during the period of the Rightly Guided Caliphate.

Umayyad and Abbasid dynasties

The next few centuries would see Islamic rule expand across empires under two main monarchies.

Umayyads

REVISED

+ The first great Muslim dynasty to rule the empire of the Caliphate with Damascus as its capital.
+ Ruled by Banu Umayya, divided between two branches of the family: the Sufyānids (661–84) and the Marwanids (684–750).
+ Conquered much of North Africa, the Middle East, South Asia and parts of Western Europe (including most of Spain and Portugal).

Abbasids

REVISED

+ Second of the two great dynasties of the Muslim Empire. The name of Banu Abbas is derived from Abbas, uncle of Muḥammad, who belonged to the Hāshimite clan.
+ Overthrew the Umayyad caliphate and slaughtered Banu Umayya en masse in Damascus, Basra, Makkah, Madinah and Yemen.
+ Reigned from 750 to 1258CE before being devasted by the Mongol invasion. The weakened Abbasid caliphate re-emerged in Cairo, Egypt, to rule there from 1261 to 1517, before being defeated by Sultan Saleem I.

Diversification of the ummah

REVISED

The expansion of these empires meant contact with new cultures and new denominations of Islam began to form. While all Muslims have always shared core beliefs and practices (for example, oneness of Allah, daily prayers), they developed different understandings about various aspects of faith.

According to the Hadith (Hadith – Ibn Majah, 3992) Muhammad knew of the divisions that would occur among his followers and stated that there would only be one rightly guided group. Several sects have claimed to be the one that would go to heaven.

Interpretations of the Qur'an

Another development and source of disagreement among Sunni and Shi'a Muslims was the approach taken to reading and making sense of the Qur'an. Although all Muslims read the same Qur'an, three main views emerged about how best to understand some of its language, specifically anthropomorphic descriptions of Allah such as references to his 'hands' (Qur'an 38: 75), 'eyes' (Qur'an 54: 14), 'face' (Qur'an 55: 27) and of his sitting on a throne (Qur'an 20: 5), which imply that Allah has a body. This raises questions such as:

+ Does Allah possess a plurality of attributes?
+ Is he simply a singular and undivided essence?
+ Can human language help make sense of his being?

The Mu`tazilites

+ Rationalist school of Islam that flourished in what is now Iraq between the eighth and tenth centuries CE and made a significant impact on Shi'a theology.
+ Believed that reason is needed to understand revelation.
+ Rejected literalist readings of such passages, arguing that Allah does not have a body and cannot be seen in this world or the next.
+ These Qur'anic references are metaphors – 'hands' for Allah's blessing or the people chosen to carry out his work, 'eyes' for his knowledge, 'face' for his essence, and sitting on his throne for omnipotence.

The Ash`arites

+ Sunni school founded by Abu al-Hasan al-Ash`ari (d. 936CE) who separated from his Mu`tazilite teachers.
+ Sceptical of rationalism, particularly the way the Mu`tazilites had employed it.
+ Maintained that these expressions represented real attributes of God, although it was not possible to fully know their precise nature.
+ Believed that Allah can show us everything that exists including himself. Therefore, the statement that 'No vision can take Him in' (Qur'an 6: 103) applies only to this world.

The Hanbalis

+ Part of the Sunni tradition, founded by Ahmad ibn Hanbal (d. 855CE), associated with the literal approach as adopted in Saudi Arabia.
+ Appear closer to the Ash`arites in accepting references to Allah as they appear in the Qur'an and the Hadith.
+ Many scholars have rejected such Hadith as weak and say that they misrepresent Imam Ahmad ibn Hanbal's own rejection of anthropomorphism.
+ Imam Al-Ghazali argued that a plurality of views and interpretations could be tolerated as long as they were not advocating a rejection of key beliefs, such as tawhid, risalah and akhirah.

Research activity

Using information from this chapter and Chapters 3, 4, 5 and 11, produce a table showing whether or not Shi'a Muslims believe in a distinct form of Islam. An example is given below to start you off.

Shi'a as distinct	Shi'a as not distinct
Do not believe in the first three Rightly Guided Caliphs	Believe in the oneness of Allah and prophethood of Muhammad

---

Sufism

+ Tasawuff is a form of Islamic mysticism. It means purifying the heart to achieve nearness to God.
+ It emphasises the role of ascetism (renouncing materialistic things) as a means of purifying oneself and developing a personal relationship with Allah.

Ascetism Renouncing materialistic things

+ Practitioners of Tasawwuf are commonly called Sufi. This is believed to be derived from the Arabic 'suf' (wool), referring to the woollen garment worn by earlier Muslim ascetics.
+ Developed as a response to the increasing materialism and departure from a proper practice of Islam, particularly under the Umayyad dynasty, in which Muslim rulers were more interested in power than piety.

Suggested answer guidance to exam practice at **www.hoddereducation.co.uk/myrevisionnotesdownloads**

- Sufism is traced back to the Qur'an and the actions of Muhammad. He is said to have been an ascetic prior to the Night of Power and has been called the 'greatest Sufi'.
- Sufism is characterised by a wide range of practices and different expressions within it, often (but not exclusively) adding acts to traditional forms of prayer such as Salah to achieve nearness to Allah.

Sufis believe that personal mystical union with Allah is possible through:
- remembrance of Allah (dhikr) – ritualised devotional acts, both liturgical (formal) and non-liturgical (informal), containing short phrases or prayers that are repeated silently or aloud, sometimes with the use of tasbih (glorification of Allah) beads. Dhikr is at the heart of Sufi practice
- self-purification (tazkiyat al-nafs) – through practices such as fasting (Sawm), prayers at night (qiyam al-layl), periods of seclusion (khalawat) and meditation (muraqaba).

> **Dhikr** The remembrance of Allah, usually associated with Sufis
>
> **Tazkiyat al-nafs** Self-purification

Sufis aim to achieve the ascent to Allah experienced by Muhammad during the Mi`raj (Qur'an 53: 1–18). They strive to reconcile living in the material world and a constant yearning to connect with Allah and establish a permanent union with him (wilayah). Shawq, or love and devotion to God, is a central feature in Sufism. For Sufis, divine love is the pinnacle of faith.

Sufis like Rabia of Basri are known for articulating the love of Allah as an intrinsic virtue – to be sought for its own sake – rather than as a hope for reward or escape from punishment: 'O God, if I am worshipping you out of fear of Your hellfire, cast me into it. And if I am worshipping you out of a desire for Your paradise, prohibit me from entering it.'

Many Sufis emphasise that the soul, like the whole of creation, is an emanation of the divine, and will ultimately be absorbed into Allah's Spirit. Losing one's identity in this process does not amount to nothingness, but an absorption into Allah's immanence and omnipresence.

Sufis have expressed these elements of their worship through poetry. Much of this poetry is in Persian and the works of great mystics like Rumi and Ferdowsi continue to have a profound impact both in and beyond Islam today.

Other methods have been more controversial, notably the use of musical instruments, incense, singing and dancing, which some Sufi branches consider necessary to fulfil the soul's longing for oneness with Allah.

Types of Sufism

REVISED

'Drunken' Sufism

The poets Rumi and Hafiz refer to being 'drunk' or 'intoxicated' with the love of God, an overwhelming feeling termed 'mast' (a Persian word). Abu Yazid (popularly known as Bayazid), who lived in the ninth century, founded the 'ecstatic' or 'drunken' school of Sufism in Persia, an expression that was considered heretical by traditional Muslims.

'Drunken' Sufism is based around the concept of fana' – annihilation of the self and one's ego to achieve oneness with Allah. The Sufi must eliminate all wants and abstain from sin. For this a Sufi master is essential. A person who attains this stage is called a wali (a saint or friend of God) and the state is termed wilayat (friendship/union).

> **Fana'** Self-annihilation or losing one's ego for the sake of Allah
>
> **Shatahat** Divinely inspired statements uttered in a state of fana' (Sufi)

Fana' has both personal and social benefits, helping an individual achieve salvation in the afterlife while also inspiring them to serve Allah's creation.

Another feature of 'drunken' Sufism is shatahat – ecstatic states and utterances, made in moments of heightened consciousness and fana'. These statements are believed to be divinely inspired in response to a powerful experience. This is also known as jazaba or majzubiyah.

A-level Religious Studies: Islam

Sober Sufism

Sufis in this tradition emphasise the goal of baqa' – permanence or persistence of the self, also termed divine eternity. This is similar to states in other faiths such as nirvana (Buddhism), salvation (Christianity) and mukhti (Sanatan/Hindu Dharma). It is the highest condition attainable, experienced by prophets and saints.

Sufis in this category argue that baqa' is superior to fana' as fana' only leads to temporary contentment. Baqa' also develops ma'rifah (knowledge of Allah) and leads to ihsan (perfection or excellence). This is the goal of Sufi practices and is achieved when seekers surrender themselves to the will of Allah.

> **Baqa'** Regeneration, permanence or persistence of the self

Tariqas

REVISED ●

Up to the ninth century, Sufis were solitary mystics. Eventually, they formed orders or schools known as tariqas, with the aim of seeking haqiqah (ultimate truth) in relation to Allah.

> **Tariqas** Sufi orders

A tariqa has Sufi masters known as murshids and sheikhs, who guide murids (disciples – literally 'desirous of Allah') towards the attainment of fana' through muraqaba (meditation), prayer and dancing. Attachment to a master is considered a prerequisite to achieving self-annihilation and therefore bay'ah (allegiance) is given to them. Some Sufis recognise a hierarchy of saints and masters, the highest being the Qutb, a spiritual leader who is believed to have a special connection with Allah and to whom obedience is necessary, and from whose guidance and love the murids benefit.

Sufi teachers have also explained parables from the Qur'an to make its teachings accessible to others. This includes the Verse of Light:

> God is the Light of the heavens and earth. His Light is like this: there is a niche, and in it a lamp, the lamp inside a glass, a glass like a glittering star, fuelled from a blessed olive tree from neither east nor west, whose oil almost gives light even when no fire touches it – light upon light – God guides whoever He will to his Light; God draws such comparisons for people; God has full knowledge of everything.

(Qur'an 24: 35, Haleem 2008)

This verse has been interpreted in multiple ways:
+ Divine light is perfect in its source, protection and radiance.
+ Prophets and their successors disseminate this light and the verses following this passage refer to the establishment of the light of Caliphs among Muslims (Qur'an 24: 55).
+ The light is the Prophet Muhammad who has been called 'nur' elsewhere (Qur'an 5: 16) and who has the purest heart. His qualities before he received revelation prepared him to deliver Allah's message to others, as signified by 'whose oil almost gives light even when no fire touches it'.
+ This is the stage murids should aspire to reach.

Whirling Dervishes

REVISED ●

One of the most famous tariqas is the Mevlevi order, based on the teachings of thirteenth-century mystic Mawlana Rumi. It is one of the largest and influential orders in Turkey and, unlike other orders, survived Ataturk's secular reforms in 1923. Members of the Mevlevi order are popularly called Whirling Dervishes as they perform a spiritual concert known as sama, during which they spin in circles to represent the planets of the solar system acting according to the will of Allah. It also symbolises the circuit of the Ka'bah. During the whirling, the dervishes point their right hand upwards towards heaven for divine blessings, point their left hand downwards to transmit the blessings down to Earth, and repeat the words 'La ilaha illAllah' (there is no god except Allah). Dervishes wear long white robes and conical hats. The sama has become an emblem of Turkish Islam.

Suggested answer guidance to exam practice at **www.hoddereducation.co.uk/myrevisionnotesdownloads**

The Song of the Reed

The Song of the Reed is among Rumi's most famous writings. It is believed that he wrote it while separated from his friend Shams Tabrizi. 'Reed' refers to a person who has reached perfection and is a metaphor for the spiritual journey to be undertaken to know Allah. It is recited in Mevlevi ritual ceremonies, accompanied by a mournful tune played on the ney flute to reflect the pain of separation.

> My inner life is not far off from my cry
> But the light to see is not in ear or eye
> Spirit's not hid from flesh nor flesh from spirit
> But none is granted leave to see the spirit.
> It's not wind, it's fire, this reed-stalk's wailing song
> Anyone who doesn't have it, won't live on

(Extract from *The Song of the Reed*, Masnavi, by Rumi)

Sufism and the wider Islamic tradition

REVISED

The relationship between Sufism and the wider Islamic tradition has been complex and contested, with Sunni and Shi'a Muslims responding differently to its teachings and practices. Sufism is not viewed as a sect or school of Islam, but an esoteric interpretation and movement within existing Muslim traditions. It is found across all branches and denominations, including Sunni and Shi'a. William Chittick says that 'Sufism is a specific approach to Islamic learning and practice that has been found among Muslims everywhere', and Ron Geaves states that 'the life of a Sufi is one that seeks to be God-permeated' which both indicate that Sufism is not independent of Islam. Various arguments are presented to support and oppose its place in Islam:

Supporters say:
- ✔ Sufi aims are based on the teachings of Islam, such as self-purification (Qur'an 91: 9–10) and friendship with Allah (Qur'an 10: 62) which are part of greater Jihad, the 'pinnacle' of faith (Hadith).
- ✔ Sufism emerged in response to the highly legalistic nature of Islam and status given to Muslim scholars who were given such importance that it was seen to be a form of shirk.
- ✔ The status of Qutb (perfect teacher) in Sufism is similar to the role of the Imams in Shi'a Islam who are considered infallible but are not worshipped.
- ✔ Sufis emphasise that it is still possible to have communion with Allah and experience revelation (ilham). Allah is not a deity who only communicated in the past.
- ✔ Sufis have made important contributions to art and literature, inspiring Muslims and non-Muslims and promoting a positive image of Islam.

Those opposed say:
- ✘ Some devotional practices, such as the use of music and dancing, were never practised by Muhammad and the early Muslims and are dangerous innovations.
- ✘ The earliest figures in Islam, including Muhammad and his successors, maintained the right balance between spirituality and worldly commitments (the first and third Caliphs, Abu Bakr and Uthman respectively, were very wealthy).
- ✘ Fana' as a practice is not one of the Five Pillars (Sunni) or Ten Obligatory Acts (Shi'a) and has limited importance compared with other Muslim duties.
- ✘ The role and reverence of Sufi masters and saints can be seen as shirk.
- ✘ Emphasis on devotional acts may detract from the study of the Qur'an, Hadith and formal Salah, which are compulsory.

A-level Religious Studies: Islam

Now test yourself

5 Describe one feature of 'drunken' Sufism and one of sober Sufism.

6 Give one argument for and one against the view that Sufism is not part of Islam.

Create a Venn diagram with three overlapping circles, showing similarities and differences between Sunni, Shi'a and Sufi Muslims.

Chapter summary

✚ Muslims were united until the death of Muhammad when a disagreement arose about who should succeed him.

✚ Sunni and Shi'a Muslims present arguments to support their views about the rightful leader based on the Qur'an and Hadith.

✚ With the expansion of Muslim empires, the ummah further diversified in its understanding and practice of particular beliefs.

✚ Sufism developed through the centuries as a personal and spiritual approach to connecting with Allah, and also became institutionalised through various tariqas.

Exam practice

It is important to end an AO2 answer with a justified conclusion. This is more effective when your essay has started with a clear thesis and you have provided arguments to support and challenge the question, followed by a brief evaluation, in each paragraph. This requires weighing up the consequences of accepting or rejecting the arguments analysed. Ensure that in your justified conclusion you:

✚ refer directly to the question

✚ use the language of the question to make it obvious that you are answering the question

✚ re-read your thesis and re-state your line of argument

✚ make a clear judgement about whether the statement is true/arguement is successful

✚ use evaluative language to make this clear, for example, 'The most effective argument in favour of this point is …'

✚ provide a specific reason for your judgement through a clear process of reasoning.

'Ali was better placed to succeed Muhammad immediately after his death.'
Evaluate this claim. [Eduqas, AO2, 30]

OR

'Islam is more united than divided.' Evaluate this claim. [Eduqas, AO2, 30]

'"Drunken" Sufism cannot lead to an experience of God.' Discuss. [OCR, AO2, 40]

Suggested answer guidance to exam practice at **www.hoddereducation.co.uk/myrevisionnotesdownloads**

7 Science

The relationship between science and Islam

Importance of learning in Islam

REVISED

This chapter summarises the importance of science in early Muslim thought and how the Qur'an's emphasis on this endeavour and duty inspired successive generations of Muslims to make invaluable contributions to scientific progress. The Qur'an and Hadith contain many instructions relating to scientific learning and urge readers to study, make critical inquiries and reflect on Allah's creation.

'Lord, increase my knowledge!' (Qur'an 20: 114, Haleem 2008)
'There are truly signs in the creation of the heavens and earth, and in the alternation of night and day, for those with understanding' (Qur'an 3: 190, Haleem 2008)
'You will not see any disparity in what the Lord of Mercy creates. Look again! Can you see any cracks? Look again! And again! Your sight will turn back to you, weak and defeated' (Qur'an 67: 3–4, Haleem 2008)
'The ink of a scholar is more sacred than the blood of a martyr' (Hadith)

The Islamic Golden Age

REVISED

The pursuit of academic excellence reached its pinnacle in the celebrated Golden Age of Islam. A little over a century after Muhammad's death, under the Abbasid caliphate, Muslims entered a ground-breaking era of discovery. With the expansion of the Islamic empire into Europe, Muslims enjoyed access to a vast range of works, especially those by ancient Greek philosophers and scientists. These were translated into Arabic and used as a basis for further study. The House of Wisdom, a library in Baghdad, is said to have boasted a collection of 1 million books, and at one point the caliphal library in Al-Andalus had 400,000 books. The largest library in Europe at the time held around 400 manuscripts.

Some popular ideas, such as Aristotle's concept of an eternal universe, were challenged through philosophical arguments inspired by the Qur'an's call to investigate creation and its origins. This challenge was taken on by the proponents of the Kalam cosmological argument (see page 106), notably by Al-Kindi and Al-Ghazali.

Some of the greatest scholars in history emerged from this environment of zeal for learning and intellectual and scientific curiosity. These people became known as 'polymaths' on account of their multiple areas of expertise. Some notable examples include:

+ Al-Biruni (973–1048CE) – contributed to calculating the circumference of the Earth to 99.7 per cent accuracy, centuries before satellites and modern measuring technology
+ Al-Khwarizmi (c. 780–c. 850CE) revolutionised arithmetic by introducing the digit 0 (sifr), and developed algebra

79

+ Ibn Sina (Avicenna) (980–1037CE) – wrote *The Canon of Medicine*, which continued to be widely used in Europe in the eighteenth century
+ Ibn al-Haytham (965–1039CE) – called the 'father of modern optics', and inventor of the first camera obscura. His work contributed to the advancement of eye surgery
+ Ibn Hayyan (721–813/816CE) – popularly known as 'the father of chemistry'. He made the first classification of chemical substances and wrote the earliest known instruction for deriving inorganic compounds from organic substances
+ Al-Razi (854–925CE) – wrote important scientific treatises on infectious disease and the first book on paediatrics
+ Omar Khayyam (1048–1131CE) – devised the Jalali solar calendar, considered even more accurate than the Gregorian calendar.

These intellectual and scientific achievements, among many others, inspired the Renaissance in Europe a few centuries later, and were instrumental in shaping the direction later taken in Western science, medicine and education. Several scholars in the West have also recognised and praised this effort. Science historian George Sarton said that from 750CE to 1100CE, Muslims 'held the world stage of sciences', and anthropologist Robert Briffault describes modern science as 'the most momentous contribution of Islamic civilisation'.

The roots of the modern scientific method can be traced to the scholars of this period. Ibn al-Haytham argued that it was wrong to trust 'writings of the ancients' and that it is the duty of all scholars to approach everything they read with scepticism. He argued that critical examination is necessary to 'avoid falling into either prejudice or leniency'. This method also came to be applied to Muslim philosophical and theological thinking.

The origin of the universe

Islamic teaching

For Muslims, the Qur'an and Hadith are the main sources of knowledge for explaining how the universe came to be.

> You merge night into day and day into night; You bring the living out of the dead and the dead out of the living; You provide limitlessly for whoever You will.

(Qur'an 3: 27, Haleem 2008)

According to the Qur'an, the heavens and the Earth were split apart into their present form. The Qur'an states that everything was created in six 'days' (Qur'an 7: 54), although elsewhere the word for 'day' (yawm) is used to mean 1,000 years (Qur'an 22: 47), and 50,000 years (Qur'an 70: 4), so this might not be literal days. Muslims also believe that Allah is not bound by time, as he is the first cause of everything, omnipotent and omniscient, without whom nothing would or could have come into existence. The Muslim reformer Abu Hamid Al-Ghazali was part of the Kalam tradition (a movement that sought to defend Islam using theological reasoning) which presented a philosophical argument about Allah being the ultimate cause of everything. This states:

+ whatever begins to exist must have a cause
+ the universe began to exist and so must have a cause
+ the cause of the universe must itself be uncaused
+ the uncaused cause is Allah.

Scientific theories

Recent advances in science and the development of new technology has enabled us to acquire a better understanding about the universe. These theories about the origins and nature of the universe have developed over time.

Steady State theory
This is the theory that the universe has always existed, has remained in the same state throughout and will continue to go on forever. The theory states that the density of matter is constant over time. This was a popular theory, particularly up to the mid-twentieth century, when the discovery of quasars disproved it. A new explanation was needed.

↓

Big Bang theory
This theory states that the universe began with an explosion of a very hot, dense mass 13.7 billion years ago. This mass began to expand as it cooled, and continues to expand. Clusters of matter inside the expanding universe formed galaxies, stars and planets, including the Earth. Evidence for this is derived from background radiation or 'ripples' in space and the observation that galaxies are moving away from us.

↓

Multiverse and Expanding/Oscillating Universe theories
Some scientists have suggested that the Big Bang was not the only event of its kind. They suggest that the universe undergoes a series of cycles, meaning that the universe goes on forever. Instead of a single Big Bang creating the whole universe, a Big Bang would start off a new phase in the cosmos and be followed by another Big Bang. This enables the universe to self-regulate and experience indefinite cycles of expansion and contraction.

Muslim responses

 REVISED

Science is defined as 'the intellectual and practical activity encompassing the systematic study of the structure and behaviour of the physical and natural world through observation and experiment' and forms the basis for many atheists to question the need for Allah to account for the universe and its origins.

Most Muslims agree that the Big Bang theory provides a sound scientific explanation for the origins of the universe. They believe that it is in harmony with the Qur'an and the case made by the Kalam Muslim philosophers that the universe had a beginning. Islamic thinkers in the Middle Ages were very interested in cosmology and the behaviour of planets and ruled out the notion of an infinite regress (going back into the past without any beginning).

Muslims point to the Qur'an as a miracle in providing details of how all life started, centuries prior to modern science making the same observations:

Muslims believe that the Qur'an …	… anticipated the science of …
The heavens and the Earth were joined together before they were divided *and* Every living thing was made from water (Qur'an 21: 30)	… the Big Bang. 'Joined together' can be interpreted to refer to the singularity, when all space and matter was compressed into a single point *and* … physiology and the understanding that water is essential for all known lifeforms
Qur'an 51: 47–8 states that Allah created the 'sky with Our power and made it vast' and spread it out: 'how well We smoothed it out!'	… the accelerating universe, discovered in 1998
Qur'an 21: 104 states that the heavens will be rolled up like a scroll, 'We shall reproduce creation just as We produced it the first time.'	… the 'Big Crunch' or 'Big Bounce', the hypothetical process by which the universe will begin to collapse back in on itself after it has expanded to its maximum extent
Qur'an, 31: 10 states that Allah 'created the heavens without any visible support', 'placed firm mountains on the earth' and 'spread all kinds of animals around it'	… findings about underwater mountains that experience limited seismic activity and … recent discoveries like the fossil field at Burgess Shale in the Canadian Rocky Mountains, which explains the origin of animal life during the Cambrian period around 540 million years ago

A-level Religious Studies: Islam

There are other claims the Qur'an makes about the universe that have not yet been confirmed by scientists, but which Muslims believe will be proven with time. These include:

Black holes

Some Muslims say the Qur'an (21: 104) appears to speak of the universe collapsing into a black hole and re-emerging from its darkness. They believe this process of creation will then start again, and therefore represents a repeated phenomenon that enables the universe to be reassembled and recreated.

However, this phenomenon cannot continue indefinitely as the emerging mass from each rebirth will reduce each time compared with the mass that it absorbed. This will continue until there is insufficient mass to collapse into another black hole. This theory has been compared to the idea of the 'Big Crunch' or 'Big Bounce' postulated by some scientists.

Extra-terrestrial life

Muslims believe that while humans have been created as the pinnacle of creation, given the vastness of the universe, there are bound to be important creatures elsewhere too. 'Among His signs is the creation of the heavens and earth and all the living creatures He has scattered throughout them: He has the power to gather them all together whenever He will'. (Qur'an 42: 29).

The use of the word 'daa-bbah' in Arabic, translated as 'living creatures', is understood to refer to intelligent, land-based beings. This can extend to those that populate heavenly bodies and follow divine guidance, like humans on Earth. The verse was revealed at a time when astronomy was in its infancy, but Muslim theologians spoke of aliens in the time of the Islamic Golden Age. Not only does this verse say that such creatures exist elsewhere, but also that intelligent creatures on Earth and elsewhere will at some stage be brought into contact with each other. Additionally, Qur'an 16: 8 states '… [He created] other things you know nothing about.'

Human origins

Islamic teachings about the creation of humans

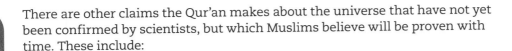

REVISED ●

> People, be mindful of your Lord, who created you from a single soul and from it created its mate, and from the pair of them spread countless men and women far and wide.

(Qur'an 4: 1, Haleem 2008)

Like Judaism and Christianity, Islam teaches the story of Adam and Hawwa (Eve). This is told in Surah Al-Baqarah (Chapter 2) and Surah Al-A'raf (Chapter 7) of the Qur'an. According to Muslim tradition, Allah moulded Adam from clay and Hawwa was made from his rib.

While many Muslims read the account of Adam and Hawwa literally, other Muslims interpret it differently. Adam is said to have been created from clay, water and dust, in the same way as Isa (Jesus) (Qur'an 3: 59) and all mortals (Qur'an 40: 67). These terms, some commentators say, apply metaphorically to the mouldable nature with which people are created and which enables them to develop particular traits. By this reasoning, Hawwa was not literally created from Adam's rib, but was of the same nature as him (Qur'an 4: 1, also see Chapter 10).

There is an internal debate in Islam about whether or not the first Adam is the same as the prophet Adam, the issue being that for the Qur'anic creation account to be scientifically accurate, they must be different people.

Suggested answer guidance to exam practice at **www.hoddereducation.co.uk/myrevisionnotesdownloads**

Theory of evolution by natural selection

The current scientific consensus about the origin of human life is based on the discoveries of nineteenth-century naturalists Alfred Russel Wallace and Charles Darwin. Both travelled extensively to study plants and animals and they observed small differences within the same species in different locations. For example, Darwin observed that finches on adjacent islands showed considerable variations in their size, beaks and claws, depending on the local food source. These observations led him to conclude that the species we observe, including humans, have not always existed in the same form, but have changed gradually over time.

According to this theory:
+ Individuals in a species show a wide range of variation, resulting from genetic differences caused by random mutations that can be inherited.
+ In most populations more offspring are produced than can survive. This leads to competition, for example, for food.
+ Individuals with characteristics most suited to their environment are more likely to survive and reproduce (survival of the fittest). The genes that allow these individuals to be successful pass to their offspring, making these specific genes more common.
+ Individuals that are poorly adapted to their environment are less likely to survive and reproduce. Consequently, their genes are less likely to be passed on.
+ Over a period of time, a species will gradually evolve.
+ Both genes and the environment can cause variation, but only genetic variation can be passed on to the next generation.
+ If two populations of one species become so different that they can no longer interbreed to form fertile offspring, this results in the formation of two species.

Darwin argued that humans have also existed in different forms in the past and that as they have similar traits to apes, humans and apes are likely to share a common ancestry. This has been substantiated by the recent discovery of other hominids (members of the family *Hominidae*, consisting of all modern and extinct humans and the great apes).

> Man in his arrogance thinks himself a great work, worthy of the interposition of a deity [God]. More humble, and I believe true, to consider him created from animals.

(Charles Darwin)

Darwin also believed human evolution would continue, saying, 'man in the distant future will be a far more perfect creature than he now is' and that the discovery of natural selection rendered the argument for a Designer God redundant.

Muslim responses

Muslim responses to Darwin's theory are divided. Some Muslim criticisms of natural selection are:
+ It doesn't seem to cohere with teachings about how humans were created instantly by Allah (Qur'an 3: 59).
+ An omnipotent being like Allah wouldn't need a process like natural selection in order to create or refine life.
+ The idea that humankind, especially the prophets, originated from earlier, 'more primitive' primates could be seen as insulting.
+ It may be hard to believe that the process of natural selection could produce the expansive diversity and complexity of life.
+ Some may feel that the process of natural selection would favour simpler life forms over complex ones, making the evolution of humans very unlikely and therefore open to doubt.

However, some, like Dr Usama Hasan, believe that natural selection is consistent with the Qur'an – although his views have been met with fierce opposition by other Muslims.

> I reply that the theory doesn't insult anyone, but does remind us of the humble origins of our created form. This is nothing new or blasphemous, since numerous Qur'anic verses remind us that we are all created from 'dust'.… Meanwhile, our spiritual form remains the most exalted.

(Usama Hasan)

According to some Muslims, the Qur'an appears to address Darwinism in accounting for how nature operates (Qur'an 28: 68). It does not discuss evolution in Darwinian terms, but as a process directed by an omniscient God. They believe that Allah has a plan for everything, therefore any form of evolution is not possible or explainable without divine agency. Nothing happens without his will and knowledge.

The Qur'an does not explicitly say that humans originated from a lower animal or form of life but does state that they underwent development through different stages.

> What is the matter with you? Why will you not fear God's majesty, when He has created you stage by stage? … how God made you spring forth from the earth like a plant.

(Qur'an 71: 13–14, 17, Haleem 2008)

The intellectual evolution of humans was articulated by Muslim scholars many centuries ago. Ibn Khaldun (1332–1406) said humans represent the apex of creation due to their rational and cognitive abilities, as well as their capacity for moral and spiritual development. Others such as the Brethren of Purity, Al Jahiz and Rumi also spoke of this.

Modern scientific writers have drawn parallels between verses in the Qur'an such as Qur'an 23: 12–14 and Qur'an 32: 9 and recent discoveries made in the field of embryology. Keith L Moore argues that the two work together and that not only does the Qur'an help us understand science, but that the science helps us understand the Qur'an in ways that were not possible before: 'We can interpret them now because the science of modern Embryology affords us new understanding.' (Keith L Moore, *The Developing Human: Clinically Orientated Embryology*). Similarly, French doctor Maurice Bucaille wrote of his amazement about how the Qur'anic revelations agree with modern scientific knowledge, a discovery that led him to 'see the Qur'an as the divinely-revealed text it really is' and become a Muslim (Maurice Bucaille, *The Qur'an and Modern Science*).

Are Islam and science compatible?

Some argue that belief in Islam is incompatible with science. Others disagree. Here are some of the arguments on both sides:

Compatible	Incompatible
The scientists of the Islamic Golden Age were hugely important. They were inspired by Qur'anic passages promoting the use of reason to understand Allah and his creation, inspiring later scientists	Muslims used to have an interest in science but after the fourteenth century, most scientific progress took place in Christian Europe and gradually Islam and science started to drift apart from each other
The Qur'an encourages investigation, enquiry and discovery rather than blind faith, and gives assurances that further knowledge will be gradually unveiled (Qur'an 15: 21)	The Qur'an says things can come into existence instantly (Qur'an 2: 117) and humans were created from clay – this is not consistent with scientific theories

Compatible	Incompatible
Muslims believe the Qur'an is a scripture for all people and all times, therefore its language had to be accessible by different individuals and societies at different periods from the seventh century onwards. Its lack of scientific language does not equate to a lack of accuracy	The Qur'an instructs Muslims to believe in its revelation and in the unseen – this is inconsistent with scientific principles and methods based on experiment and observation
A lack of knowledge about things does not invalidate their existence as they can be verified in the future. Muslims believe divine revelation is a source of knowledge and granted to those Allah chooses (Qur'an 2: 255)	Some Muslims have rejected the scientific approach and been reluctant to engage with science. The Nizamiyya schools under Nizam al-Mulk in the Seljuk dynasty shifted towards a focus on religious learning at the expense of independent inquiry
How could an illiterate man like the Prophet Muhammad in the Arab desert in the seventh century have known or guessed things that were confirmed under scientific scrutiny centuries later?	Muslims believe that the Qur'an is the revealed truth and put it above any scientific claims or theories
The Qur'an reflects so many modern scientific theories, it is irrational to ignore it	There is scientific evidence for the Big Bang and evolution by natural selection, but not for God
Scientific theories can and do change (for example, Big Bang as opposed to an eternal universe) but religious truths do not. It is possible that as scientific thought develops, it will continue to validate the teachings of the Qur'an	
The word of Allah (Qur'an) and work of Allah (universe) must be in harmony	That the Qur'an has proven to be right in matters relating to the universe does not mean that Islam as a whole is scientifically valid (the Qur'an is not a book of science)
Some Muslims welcome scientific developments such as genetic engineering on ethical grounds as long as it is used responsibly and for social benefit, such as enhancing agricultural produce and protecting it against diseases	Other Muslims oppose genetic engineering on ethical grounds as they believe it is playing God and changing the creation of Allah, showing Islam to be more invested in belief than scientific advancement
Science has many limitations and cannot go further than empiricism and therefore is not yet fully able to account for where matter emerged, the nature of consciousness or even what it means to be human. Yet these are areas the Qur'an does address	Interpretations of the Qur'an play catch-up to science, rather than leading scientific enquiry. When scientific understanding changes, the interpretation of the Qur'an changes
Only 5% of the known universe is detectable; the rest is dark matter and dark energy, yet we do not doubt that it is real. Why cannot the same principle be applied to God?	

Some Muslims argue that it's not simply a case of Science vs Faith, but that different questions require different methods of investigation. For instance, telescopes would not be used for observing the inner workings of cells, nor can a Geiger counter help with assessing earthquake activity. In the same way, Allah cannot be proven through laboratory experiments.

There is now a resurgence in Muslim interest in the sciences. For example, Professor Abdus Salam made an important contribution towards the discovery of the subatomic Higgs Boson particle (also called the 'God particle') present at the Big Bang. He received the Nobel Prize for Physics in 1979 and has been described as 'one of the greatest physicists of the last 100 years, anywhere in the world' (Jim Al-Khalili). Professor Salam attributed his scientific achievements to the Qur'an because of its emphasis on the laws of nature. He pointed out that 750 verses of the Qur'an (almost one-eighth) 'exhort believers to study nature, to reflect, to make the best use of reason in their search for the ultimate and to make the acquiring of knowledge and scientific comprehension part of the community's life' (Professor Abdus Salam speech at the UNESCO House in Paris on 27 April 1984).

Seyyed Hossein Nasr has also spoken of the importance of science in contemporary Islam as being rooted in the Qur'an: 'In Islam the inseparable link between man and nature, and also between the sciences of nature and religion, is to be found in the Qur'an itself.'

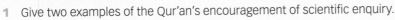

Now test yourself

TESTED ⦿

1 Give two examples of the Qur'an's encouragement of scientific enquiry.
2 Explain two points in favour of and two points against the view that Islam and science are compatible.

Chapter summary

✦ The Islamic Golden Age was a period in which Muslims excelled in learning and made extensive scientific advancements
✦ Many passages of the Qur'an accord with modern scientific theories such as about the origins of the universe
✦ There are different Muslim understandings about the creation of humans and evolution
✦ The compatibility between Islam and science continues to be debated, with many non-Muslim scientists expressing amazement with the Qur'an's accuracy about scientific discoveries

Exam practice

Examine Muslim responses to Darwin's theory of evolution. [AQA, AO1, 10]

To what extent has science had an impact on Islamic thought? [OCR, AO2, 40]

'Islamic teachings about creation are compatible with the Big Bang theory.'
Evaluate this view. [Eduqas, AO2 (A-level), 30; Pearson Edexcel, AO1 and AO2, 30]

Explain the relationship between Islam and science. [AQA, AO1, 10]

Suggested answer guidance to exam practice at **www.hoddereducation.co.uk/myrevisionnotesdownloads**

8 Ethics

Muslims get guidance from a variety of sources which form the basis of shari`a (see Chapter 3). Shari`a covers every aspect of Muslim conduct, both private and public. This chapter explains the categories for Muslim ethical action, the place of sanctity of life in Islam and Muslim approaches to crime and punishment.

The five ethical categories

So accept whatever the Messenger gives you, and abstain from whatever he forbids you.

(Qur'an 59: 7, Haleem 2008)

To help Muslims apply the principles of shari`a to their daily lives, Islamic scholars identified categories of behaviour and action which are binding on every Muslim old enough to understand them.

1 Fard

Obligatory actions which will be rewarded by Allah if observed (and attract punishment if they are not observed), such as:
+ performing Salah, fasting, giving Zakah and performing the Hajj
+ fulfilling obligations to the community
+ observing laws about the preparation of food
+ repayment of debts
+ modest behaviour and dress.

2 Mustahab

Recommended or preferred actions, rewarded by Allah, including:
+ voluntary prayers.

3 Mubah

Permitted actions, such as:
+ choice of clothing
+ where to live
+ political affiliations
+ playing sports.

4 Makruh

Disliked actions, such as:
+ bragging about financial success
+ gossip
+ sleeping late in the morning (without a valid reason)
+ becoming distracted during prayer.

5 Haram

Forbidden actions, including:
+ eating forbidden meat such as pork
+ drinking alcohol
+ gambling
+ adultery
+ murder
+ anything that promotes shirk.

> The categories are not always absolute. For example, it is fard for an adult to fast during Ramadan, but a menstruating or pregnant or breastfeeding woman is forbidden to do so. Eating pork is haram but is permitted in a life-threatening situation when there is no other food available.

A famous Hadith is that 'The reward of deeds depends on the intentions' (Hadith – Sahih al-Bukhari), indicating that Allah does not look only at the action but also the niyyah (intentions) behind them. This suggests that there is an element of personal discretion in understanding and applying shari`a.

Changing circumstances can make it difficult to apply the five categories. For example, issues like euthanasia and genetic engineering are not explicitly referred to in any primary source. Muslim scholars apply the key principles of shari`a to decide, but as this is a work of interpretation, there can be disagreements.

This has led to debates about whether the five categories are a recipe for confusion rather than clarity.

Confusion	Clarity
+ Some actions are acceptable at some times and not at others. This makes it difficult to follow the rules without constantly seeking advice + If there are disagreements, which scholars should Muslims listen to? Who has greater authority and should have the final say?	+ 'Grey' areas allow for the use of ijtihad, without which shari`a would be too rigid. Muhammad said that religion should be made 'easy' and allow flexibility + The categories have been established for centuries. They have been developed to give clarity and to avoid confusion. Most common actions have been covered

Now test yourself TESTED

1 Which category would the following fall under:
   a) Tahajjud (night prayer), b) joining a gym, c) Zakah, d) worshipping statues?

Sanctity of life

In Islam, the concept of the sanctity of life is the belief that human beings have been created by Allah with a special status and purpose. Human life is precious and must be protected and preserved. Suicide is forbidden (Qur'an 4: 29) and the murder of a single innocent life has been compared to slaughtering the whole of humanity, while saving a person is akin to saving all people (Qur'an 5: 32). Mankind has been described as a 'community' (Qur'an 23: 52) to emphasise that the human race is one.

Now test yourself TESTED

2 Give two examples of Muslim teachings that describe the sanctity of life.

Suggested answer guidance to exam practice at **www.hoddereducation.co.uk/myrevisionnotesdownloads**

The embryo and unborn child

The status of unborn children is a sensitive and controversial issue. Many legal and moral arguments are made about whether or when a foetus has rights. Some have devised criteria for personhood, including capacity for consciousness, reasoning and communication, to determine at which point an embryo can be considered a human. This is often used to apply to foetuses, particularly surrounding decisions about issues like abortion.

An abortion is the deliberate ending of a pregnancy and is allowed under UK law under certain conditions. The 1967 Abortion Act and amendments to this in the Human Fertilisation and Embryology Act of 1990 allow abortions in the first 24 weeks of pregnancy if two doctors agree that:
+ the mother's life is at risk
+ the unborn child would be severely disabled
+ there is a risk to the mother's physical or mental health

or
+ any existing children would suffer or be at risk.

Abortion is allowed after 24 weeks if either of the first two conditions above are met or to prevent permanent injury to the pregnant woman.

Muslim attitudes

Muslims are pro-life. They believe that all life is a gift from Allah and therefore sacred, and it is not for humans to interfere in his plan for any individual.

> it is He who gives death and life

(Qur'an 53: 44, Haleem 2008)

According to a Hadith, life begins when an angel blows the breath of life into the foetus. This is called ensoulment and takes place 120 days after conception.

Most Muslims believe that if a pregnancy endangers the mother's health, her life takes precedence and an abortion is therefore acceptable. According to the Qur'an, financial difficulties should never be a reason for terminating a pregnancy, as Allah provides for people's needs if they seek his help (Qur'an 17: 31).

Additionally, Muslims are taught that:
+ every embryo has the potential for life and should therefore have a right to be born
+ just because a baby might be disabled, does not mean it cannot live a decent life
+ giving a baby up for adoption is a better option than abortion
+ children are a blessing, not a burden.

Now test yourself　　　　　　　　　　TESTED

3　Give two Muslim beliefs about the status of an unborn child.

Stewardship and the environment

The Qur'an says that humans have been made khalifahs ('caliphs' or stewards) of the Earth, entrusted with a duty to care for Allah's creation:

It is He who made you successors on the earth.

(Qur'an 6: 165, Haleem 2008)

Muslims believe that humans are the pinnacle of creation and are responsible for protecting and preserving the environment. This is particularly important now that climate change has become one of the most pressing issues facing the world. Other environmental issues such as pollution, animal extinction and the draining of natural resources, are also major concerns.

Muslims believe that, as caliphs, they have a duty to use the Earth's resources sustainably, and to maintain the harmony and balance that Allah created at the start of creation. Each generation is responsible for ensuring that the next can also enjoy Allah's bounties. Allah will judge us on how we treat the Earth. This is an important role of the ummah.

Many Muslims support conservation projects and recycling, having been inspired by the teachings of the Qur'an and Hadith.

> *There is none amongst the Muslims who plants a tree or sows seeds, and then a bird, or a person or an animal eats from it, but is regarded as a charitable gift for him.*
>
> (Hadith – Bukhari 39: 513)
>
> The Islamic Foundation for Ecology and Environmental Sciences (IFEES) collaborates with many organisations worldwide to help protect the environment. Muslims for Humanity is a scheme to help provide volunteers to plant more trees around the UK. So far they have planted 240,000 trees.

Animals

Muslims believe that Allah created animals for an important purpose and that they should be treated with respect.

Muslims are taught to avoid:
+ over-working or over-loading animals
+ neglecting animals
+ hunting animals for sport
+ animal fighting as a sport
+ factory farming.

Most Muslims believe that animal experimentation is acceptable as long as the animals do not suffer, and if it benefits humanity – such as for the development of medicine – but oppose experimenting on animals for luxuries such as cosmetics.

Food

For meat to be halal (permissible), the ritual slaughter (dhabihah) must take place according to strict guidelines, some of which are designed to minimise the suffering of the animal.
+ Animals must be fed and watered before they are killed.
+ The slaughter must involve a clean cut to the animal's throat, made as swiftly and humanely as possible.
+ Animals should not be shown the knife or be slaughtered in front of other animals, as this would cause them distress.
+ Animals should not be stunned before slaughter as Muslims believe this causes more pain and distress to the animal and may kill the animal before it is slaughtered, making it haram. However, some Muslims accept stunning if there is sufficient supervision to prove that the animal (especially poultry) is still alive after being stunned. Larger animals such as cows and sheep are unlikely to die due to stunning.

Research activity

Create a list of jobs a caliph (steward) would be expected to carry out as part of their responsibilities to the environment and animal life.

Now test yourself

4 Write down three rules of ritual slaughter.

Suggested answer guidance to exam practice at **www.hoddereducation.co.uk/myrevisionnotesdownloads**

Crime and punishment

Traditional Muslim views

Muslims believe that a system of law and order is needed in society to keep people safe. Without justice or a criminal system, there would be unrest.

Justice is:
+ commanded by Allah (Qur'an 4: 58)
+ upheld by all prophets (Qur'an 57: 25)
+ next to taqwa or God-consciousness (Qur'an 5: 8).

Muslims therefore strive to stand up for what is fair. However, Islam forbids Muslims from taking the law into their own hands to achieve this purpose.

Muslims believe laws should be respected and followed, regardless of whether they are based on the principles of shari`a or another legal system (see Chapter 11). Islam prescribes particular punishments for those who consciously break religious and civil laws. These aim to serve the best interests of the offender, victim and wider society. Punishment should be fair and proportionate to the crime committed. In Islam, many crimes would also be classified as sins (as they go against Allah's will).

The three categories of crimes are:
1 **Hudud** – crimes against God, which have a fixed punishment based on the Qur'an, Sunnah and Hadith. Examples include adultery, alcohol consumption and armed robbery.
2 **Qisas** – crimes against individuals or families, where the criminal must make up for the offence. In the case of murder, the victim's nearest relatives can choose their preferred course of action. This could be retaliatory (capital punishment), compensatory (payment of diyya, or blood money) or reconciliatory (forgiveness).
3 **Ta'zir** – crimes for which punishment is not stated in the Qur'an or Hadith and is decided by a qadi (judge). Examples include inappropriate behaviour such as encouraging lying which may be punished with corporal punishment, a prison sentence or a fine.

Punishments for these crimes can only be carried out in countries that are governed according to the shari'a. Few Muslim states use ta'zir today – Brunei applies it with adult Muslims who miss Friday prayers and Iran does so in the case of financial corruption.

Capital punishment

Capital punishment is also known as the death penalty. A number of countries including China, the Democratic Republic of Congo, Iran, Nigeria, Pakistan, Saudi Arabia and the USA use it to punish serious crimes, such as murder or treason. The Qur'an gives commandments regarding the use of capital punishment under the law of qisas:

> Do not take life, which God has made sacred, except by right. This is what He commands you to do.

(Qur'an 6: 151, Haleem 2008)

Qisas aims to provide an effective and practical means to safeguard human life. If a person shows callous disregard for the life of another person or behaves threateningly towards others, they may lose their right to remain a member of society, unless those directly affected choose to accept monetary compensation or forgive them.

According to Qur'anic teachings:

+ proportionate punishments are to be given to offenders, without distinction, as all are equal before the law: 'The blood, wealth and honour of the Muslim are sacred to all Muslims.' (Hadith – Sahih Muslim)
+ the death penalty is not always necessary. Relatives of a murder victim have the option to forgive the murderer, with or without the payment of blood money
+ the use of the word 'brother' (Qur'an 2: 178) reminds believers of their shared faith and encourages leniency. However, murderers must pay blood money without delay if demanded. This serves as a reminder that offenders will not always be forgiven.

These guidelines are important as they prevent the victim's family trying to take vengeance. Qisas is seen as striking a balance between justice and mercy.

Traditionalist, modernist and non-Muslim scholarly views

Traditionalist scholar	Egyptian Sunni scholar Sheikh Ahmad Ash-Sharabasi supports the death penalty, arguing that it is a form of self-defence. He believes that society should fight back against criminals who attack the rule of law. The Qur'an only appears to allow the death penalty in cases of murder and crimes against the community.
	'All lawmakers legalize self-defence and they say it is permissible for one to kill a person who attacks him, if there is no other way. [...] So when the society calls for death penalty for such a criminal, it is really in a state of self-defence.' (Ahmad Ash-Sharabasi – Al Azhar University)
Modernist scholar	Swiss Muslim academic Tariq Ramadan advocates a suspension of capital punishment across the Islamic world so that a review can be carried out by scholars. He believes that change will not happen overnight and it is important to be practical and patient when debating the issue with Muslim leaders who still authorise death sentences.
	'Considering that the opinions of most scholars … are neither explicit nor unanimous … and the state of the majority Muslim societies do not guarantee a just and equal treatment of individuals before the law, it is our moral obligation and religious responsibility to demand for the immediate suspension of the application of the hudud which is inaccurately accepted as an application of Islamic Shari'a.' (Tariq Ramadan)
Non-Muslim scholar	American academic James Rachels endorses utilitarian principles that work best for society overall rather than adherence to any fixed laws. He believes that an 'eye for an eye' approach makes punishers no better than the criminals.
	'When a rational being decides to treat people in a certain way, he [decides] that this is how people are to be treated. Thus if we treat him the same way in return, we are doing nothing more than treating him as he has decided to be treated. If he treats others badly, and we treat him badly, we are complying with his own decision.' (James Rachels)

Most Muslims believe that punishment should not be designed to make an individual suffer, but to create a better and safer society for all, linking to Islam's aim of establishing peace at all levels. Some punishments may appear harsh but very strict conditions must apply for them to take place and more lenient options are provided as alternatives (for example, monetary compensation).

Are Islamic teachings on punishment applicable today?

REVISED

Applicable today	Not applicable today
Many Muslims believe that the teachings of the Qur'an and Hadith are for all times and therefore more important than other laws	There was only one case of stoning in 623 years of the Ottoman empire, while Iran and Saudi Arabia carry out multiple executions every year, raising questions about the inconsistency of its application by Muslims

Suggested answer guidance to exam practice at **www.hoddereducation.co.uk/myrevisionnotesdownloads**

Applicable today	Not applicable today
Many interpretations consider Islamic rulings about crime and punishment to be consistent with the spirit of other legal systems and human rights laws	Others see conflict between Islamic teachings and bodies like the United Nations (for example, use of the death penalty, which the UN opposes)
Teachings in the Qur'an and Sunnah encourage forgiveness more than justice, and interventions to stop people being punished often succeed (for example, when a British primary teacher in Sudan was accused of blasphemy and jailed for allowing her class to name a teddy bear 'Muhammad'; she was later released)	The Prophet Muhammad was often averse to authorising punishment (for example, he kept turning away from a person who had admitted committing adultery, preferring the individual to repent rather than seek punishment)
There are strict conditions for hudud punishments, making them difficult and rare (for example, four witnesses to an act of adultery – Qur'an 24: 4). There has to be 100% proof that the crime was committed	Endorsement of capital punishment in some Muslim countries has led to individuals taking the law into their own hands and murdering people they consider to be apostates and blasphemers (for example, Ahmadiyya Muslims in Pakistan)
Hudud, qisas and ta'zir are only applicable in Muslim countries. Hudud crimes apply when people's behaviour affects public order and safety (for example, social disturbance due to alcohol)	

Now test yourself TESTED

5 Name the three types of crime and give an example for each.

6 Summarise in one sentence each a traditionalist, modernist and non-Muslim view of capital punishment.

7 'Islam puts compassion before consequences.' Write down two points for and two points against this statement.

Research activity

Create a spider diagram with 'Capital punishment' in the centre and add four or five Muslim beliefs about it.

Chapter summary

+ Muslims believe in five categories of ethical action: fard, mustahab, halal, makruh and haram.
+ Sanctity of life and stewardship are important concepts in Islam and determine the approach Muslims take to issues such as the status of the embryo and unborn child, the environment and the treatment of animals.
+ There are modernist and traditionalist approaches to how crimes should be punished in Islam.

Exam practice

Explain the five categories of ethical action as a framework for Muslim living.
[Eduqas, AO1, (AS), 25]

Examine the responsibilities of the ummah as Khalifah (stewards) towards the environment. [AQA, AO1, 10]

'Islamic teachings on punishment cannot be applied today.' Evaluate this view.
[Eduqas, AO2, 30]

Write an introductory thesis for this question. Here are some tips to help you:
+ Define your terms: Are there any words in the question which need explaining? If the question asks you to compare, how will you define success?
+ Implications: Why is this question important? This helps you to show the examiner your grasp of what the question is asking.
+ Scholars: Who are the key scholars involved in this debate? Do you know the names of their works or articles they have written? Use them!
+ Thesis: You need to show what your conclusion is going to be right at the beginning. You must clearly state and justify the line of argument you are going to pursue throughout the essay from the start.

9 Gender and feminism in Islam

Gender roles and women's rights are among the most debated areas in Islam. This chapter outlines the important contributions made by female Muslims since the time of Muhammad and both traditional and changing Muslim attitudes about the family. Additionally, you will learn about the impact of secularism, the ways that Muslim thought have been influenced by the West and the work of feminists within Islam.

Gender in scripture and early Islam

Muslims believe Islam to be a complete way of life and a comprehensive code for living. Society started with the creation of man and woman:

> People, be mindful of your Lord, who created you from a single soul, and from it created its mate, and from the pair of them spread countless men and women far and wide.

(Qur'an 4: 1, Haleem 2008)

Men and women have been created with a given 'form' (Qur'an 20: 50) in ways that help achieve God's plan and purpose for them. Gender roles in Islam are broadly similar, but there are distinct elements. These are so that the responsibilities given to men and women help achieve peace, both in the home and society as a whole (see Family life – page 96 – and interpretation of Surah 4: 34 – page 99). Harmony in the world is not possible without harmony in the home, which is why Muhammad taught: 'The best of you is the one who behaves best towards your women [mothers, wives, daughters and so on]' (Hadith – Sunan al-Tirmidhi).

Spiritual equality REVISED

In addition to highlighting the joint role of husbands and wives in raising good families, the Qur'an also emphasises that men and women are spiritually equal before Allah. Both are promised that their righteous deeds will be rewarded (Qur'an 3: 195) and 'will not be wronged' (Qur'an 4: 124).

The Qur'an (33: 35) lists ten levels of faith by, for instance, dressing modestly, fasting and giving to charity, and states repeatedly that these can be achieved by both men and women.

> **Now test yourself**   TESTED
>
> 1   Give one example from the Qur'an where men and women are described as spiritually equal.

Women in early Islam

Women have always played a central role in Islam and the consolidation and spread of the ummah. From those who demonstrated the highest level of devotion at the time of Muhammad, to intellectuals who have advanced science and culture, women's contributions to the development of Islam have been indispensable.

Prominent early examples include:

+ the wives of Muhammad, called 'mothers' of the believers (Qur'an 33: 6), including:
    + Khadija – Muhammad's first wife, who supported him, financially and emotionally, particularly during the earliest part of his prophethood
    + Aishah – one of the most common narrators of Hadith and earliest scholars of Islam, from whom Muhammad said Muslims could learn half the faith
    + Hafsa – helped with the preservation of the Qur'an and was responsible for the safe-keeping of its compilation, which was used by the third Caliph, Uthman, when the Qur'an was being standardised (see Chapter 3)
+ Muhammad's daughter Fatimah, who is counted by Shi'a Muslims as one of the fourteen 'infallibles' (immune from sins and mistakes), along with her father and the twelve Imams
+ Sumayyah – among the first believers and martyrs in Islam
+ Khawlah bint al-Azwar – female warrior in the early battles of Islam, after whom many schools, streets and military units in Muslim countries are named
+ Umm al-Darda – seventh-century scholar who taught jurisprudence in the mosques of Damascus and Jerusalem, whose students included men and women
+ Fatima Al-Fihri – founder of the world's oldest degree-granting university, the University and Mosque of Al Quaraouiyine, Morocco, in 859.

> Muhammad said of Khadija, 'She believed in me when no one else did; she accepted Islam when people rejected me; and she helped and comforted me when there was no one else to lend me a helping hand.'

(Hadith – Sahih al-Bukhari)

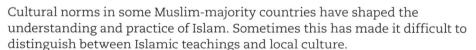

Now test yourself TESTED

2 Name any three important women in early Islam and give a brief description of their contributions.

Traditional views

Cultural norms in some Muslim-majority countries have shaped the understanding and practice of Islam. Sometimes this has made it difficult to distinguish between Islamic teachings and local culture.

Some practices that oppress women can be linked to local tradition that pre-existed Islam. While the Qur'an advocates gender equality, this has been challenging to implement in societies that have embraced Islam but remain under the strong influence of cultural norms or extreme applications of shari'a, such as forced marriages and the denial of education to girls.

There is huge diversity of thought and practice in relation to hijab, from those who wear the niqab (face veils) and chador (cloaks) outside the home (for example, in Afghanistan, Iran) to those who choose not to cover their heads at all.

Female genital mutilation (FGM) is often associated with Islam, particularly in Africa, Yemen and other Middle Eastern and Asian countries. It is practised in these countries, but it was a part of the culture before Islam was practised, and is practised there by non-Muslims too.

In most Muslim-majority countries, Muslim women must marry Muslim men, however this is starting to change: in 2017, Tunisia allowed Muslim women to marry non-Muslim men (under Tunisian secular law, rather than in shari`a courts) despite the country being 99 per cent Muslim.

With respect to education, historically in the Muslim world it is mainly men who have attended higher education institutions and acquired the highest academic qualifications. Again, there are exceptions, such as in Algeria where more women attend and graduate from university than men.

Family life

The Qur'an and Hadith teach that men and women have clearly defined purposes and were made to complement each other. Muslims believe that these roles work together best when two people have made a lifelong commitment in marriage. Marriage is sacred and the foundation of Muslim family life. In a Hadith, Muhammad said religion is the most important quality in a spouse and Muslims are encouraged to marry within their faith.

> When a man has married, he has completed one half of his religion, so let him fear Allah with regard to the other half.

(Hadith – Sunan al-Bayhaqi)

For Muslims, family life is the cornerstone of society. Married Muslim couples are expected to have children if they are able, as procreation is a key purpose of marriage and children are seen as a blessing. Many Muslims have large families. Muslims believe that the proper raising of children is extremely important and is a way of passing on values that will strengthen the ummah as well as ensuring that they become good citizens who contribute positively to society.

Muslims are taught that there should be love and kindness between members of the family at all levels. Parents are given particular importance and respect (Qur'an 4: 36), especially mothers because of the suffering they experience during pregnancy and childbirth: 'We have commanded man to be good to his parents: his mother struggled to carry him and struggled to give birth to him.' (Qur'an 46: 15).

Mothers have been given a high status and Allah is pleased when people respect and care for their mothers: 'Paradise lies at the feet of your mothers' (Hadith – Sunan al-Nasa'i).

Muslims believe teachings like these highlight the central place given by Allah to family life in Islam and provide the key to achieving a happy, healthy and harmonious home.

Roles of men and women

REVISED ●

Some roles in a family are shared, such as being loyal to each other; men and women are also described as 'garments' (Qur'an 2: 187) for one another (i.e. to comfort and protect each other). Other roles are specific to men or women.

The role of men	The role of women
+ Acting as breadwinners and supporting the family – providing a home, paying bills and covering other costs of daily living (Qur'an 4: 34) + Treating their wives with kindness, as equals and being faithful to them (Qur'an 4: 19) + Helping with the running of the household as modelled by the Prophet – this is not to be left entirely to women (Qur'an 33: 21)	+ Being a wife and mother (the most important role of a woman, in accordance with the nature given to her by Allah – Qur'an 20: 50) + Being faithful to their husbands (Qur'an 4: 34) + Running the home, educating their children in Islam and teaching them morality

Suggested answer guidance to exam practice at **www.hoddereducation.co.uk/myrevisionnotesdownloads**

The ummah is seen as a family for all Muslims, who refer to each other as brothers and sisters, and are taught to look out for and help each other. For Shi'a Muslims, there is a special place for the ahl al-bayt or family of the Prophet Muhammad who have divine right authority to teach Islam. They are seen as the ideal family in Islam whose example is to be followed.

Changing roles

REVISED

In recent times, the changing landscape of society has meant that some Muslims have changed their attitudes to the roles of men and women in the family. Better access to education, career opportunities and social interactions have meant that young people are more independent, and women especially are less reliant on their families to find a husband for them. Muslim women increasingly have careers that mean that some of them feel they do not need a husband to provide for them. Many married Muslim women now earn as much as their husbands and are able to share the burden of supporting the family finances. This means that men feel less pressured by the role of breadwinner and are grateful for the financial support of their wives in maintaining the home and the opportunity to be involved in other aspects of family life.

Now test yourself

TESTED

3   How are the roles of husband and wife in Islam:
    a) similar
    b) different?

Secularity and contact with the West

Over the centuries, Muslims have settled in different parts of the world, especially in secular societies. This has inevitably influenced developments in Muslim thinking. For instance, living under the British Empire in India led to Muslim figures like Sayyid Ahmad Khan (d. 1898) wanting to incorporate the benefits of British education and ideas into a new modern Islam.

Since the mid-nineteenth century, campaigns for gender equality have led to increased rights for women in secular societies, securing their access to the vote, higher education and employment and property rights – rights already given by Islam to women thirteen centuries earlier. These changes have affected the way women are perceived and treated in society. Women are represented in most professions and a third of British MPs are women. In some households, women bring in most or all of the income and a small but increasing number of men have assumed the role of stay-at-home dads.

Now test yourself

TESTED

4   Give two examples of changes to the rights of women in secular societies.

Contemporary views of marriage, divorce and celibacy

Muslims believe that:

+ sex is only permitted within marriage and its primary purpose is reproduction
+ the process of getting married means the relationship is taken more seriously
+ they should marry within their faith
+ they should not date and should involve their families in selecting a spouse, but it remains the man and woman's decision to accept or reject a marriage proposal.

Although most Muslims still follow this approach, some embrace the diversity of Western society and:

+ marry non-Muslims from among the People of the Book (such as monotheistic followers of Judaism and Christianity) and different racial backgrounds
+ choose their own partner, using match-making sites and apps, rather than asking their families
+ date before marriage, as long as they intend it to lead to marriage (though this is regarded as haram).

In Islam, divorce is seen as breaking a link that Allah created. However, divorce is allowed in cases of:

+ a husband abandoning his wife
+ impotency and infertility
+ apostasy (leaving Islam)
+ abuse
+ infidelity.

Marriage is my sunnah. Those who do not follow my sunnah do not belong to me.

(Hadith – Bukhari)

Of all the things Allah has made lawful, He hates divorce the most.

(Hadith – Abu Dawud)

Celibacy is not allowed in Islam. Muslims believe that sex is a gift to be valued in marriage and consider it part of human nature given by God. Married couples benefit from fulfilling this natural need in a halal way.

> **Now test yourself**
>
> 5 Write down three purposes of marriage in Islam.
>
> TESTED

Contemporary views of homosexuality and transgender issues

The legalisation of same-sex marriages in England and Wales in 2013 and the widening of transgender rights has posed challenges to Muslim communities.

+ The Qur'an and Hadith regard homosexuality as interfering with Allah's plan for humanity to procreate. This makes same-sex relationships unnatural and therefore sinful.
+ Some Muslims accept that some people are naturally gay and believe rejecting this leads to intolerance.
+ Most Muslims view transgenderism as changing Allah's creation and therefore sinful. They believe that both homosexuality and transgenderism are choices people make that need to be resisted, as they go against God's plan.
+ Muslims who have these views maintain that this is not an excuse to discriminate against gay and trans people – all people should be treated with respect regardless of their sexual or gender orientation.

> **Now test yourself** TESTED
>
> 6 Give brief summaries of the contemporary Muslim views on celibacy, marriage, homosexuality and transgender issues.

Suggested answer guidance to exam practice at **www.hoddereducation.co.uk/myrevisionnotesdownloads**

Feminism and equality

The rise of feminism, both in the Muslim world and the West, has influenced Muslim thought on the role and status of women in Islam. Many feminist scholars have focused on challenging what are seen as patriarchal forces that have denied women equality, and restoring women's rights as granted by the Qur'an and the Prophet Muhammad fourteen centuries ago. Their work has been met with varying responses and success within Islam.

Professor Aisha Abd Al Rahman

REVISED

+ Writing under the name Bint ash Shati (daughter of the riverbank), her pioneering work led her to be described as Egypt's leading female Islamic writer and scholar.
+ She raised awareness of the need for gender equality through writing and lectures focused on women in the life of Muhammad and the teachings of the Qur'an.
+ Her first novel, *The Sinned Woman* (1953), was about social injustices and the suffering of women and was later turned into a screenplay.
+ She did not support modern feminist movements. She argued that 'the equal, instinctual woman admits that man has a legal and natural right to guardianship over her', but that this did not affect women's rights to equality in education, inheritance, property ownership and pursuit of a career, which Islam had already given fourteen centuries ago.
+ She said that society's failure to value of the role of mothers was 'a major stumbling block … for which our generation paid a terrible price.'

Haleh Afshar

REVISED

+ Born in Iran, she is a founding member of the Muslim Women's Network and author of numerous books on Islam and feminism including *Islam and Feminisms: An Iranian Case Study*. She is also an advisor to the United Nations on women's issues.
+ She argues that women had important roles to play in early Islam and are entitled to interpret the Qur'an and Hadith independently, and that no understanding can be imposed on anyone. She cites Qur'anic passages proving that women are equal to men, including, 'The believers, both men and women, support each other.' (Qur'an 9: 71).

For far too long the domain of Islamic law had been controlled by men; but gradually women and their male allies are making a bid to change this process. They too have returned to the sources … to come to rather different conclusions from the traditionalists.

The interpretation of Surah 4: 34

REVISED

A controversial passage in the Qur'an relating to the status and treatment of women is in Surah Al-Nisa.

Throughout the history of Islam this Surah has sometimes been interpreted to mean that men are permitted to beat women, and so some people still believe that this Surah justifies violence.

However, many Muslims believe that the original Arabic provides context which allows for different interpretations. The Arabic word 'nushuz' (translated as high-handedness, disloyalty or ill-conduct), when used about a person, means any evil conduct including violence (in this case, on the part of the wife). Therefore, this could have been intended to refer only to a man's right to defend himself against his wife's physical aggression.

Others point out that the Surah says that physical force should not be the norm but has to be a last resort. A husband must first exercise patience; if the problem persists, he is to avoid sleeping or talking with her; only if there is still no change to his wife's aggressive behaviour, is he permitted to use minimal physical force.

The Surah also reminds both parties that Allah is above them and will hold them responsible for their actions. As the Qur'an advises peaceful relations and kind treatment even in difficult domestic situations (Qur'an 25: 63, 4: 19), and Muhammad condemned men who beat their wives (Hadith – Kathir), most Muslims do not believe that this Surah excuses violence.

> **Now test yourself**   TESTED ◯
>
> 7   According to Surah 4: 34, what three steps should be taken by a husband if his wife is guilty of 'nushuz'?

Amina Wadud   REVISED ●

Historically, only men have led prayers when men and women make up the congregation. All prophets, caliphs (Sunni) and imams (Shi'a) have been men, and today it is mainly men who have leading roles in mosques and the wider Muslim community. While women can lead other women in prayer, this is rarely the case when men are present.

In 2008, the Muslim Educational Centre of Oxford invited Amina Wadud, a female American scholar, to lead both men and women in Friday prayers.

> There is nothing in the Qur'an that prohibits it. My own theological research into the essence of Islam indicates the necessity for us to be able to move away from the tradition that restricted women from the practice of leading prayer.

(Amina Wadud)

Some saw this as progressive and similar to women taking leading political roles in Muslim-majority countries, such as Benazir Bhutto (Pakistan), Megawati Sukarnoputri (Indonesia) and Masoumeh Ebtekar (Iran). Others argue that there are practical challenges to women leading a community of believers due to the observance of hijab and segregation between men and women. As women are prohibited from entering a mosque and praying during menstruation, this also poses a problem. Others say that leadership in religion and in secular society are different and cannot be compared. The Qur'an states that women, like men and children, can be 'imams' in the sense of being good examples of virtue (Qur'an 25: 74).

Hijab   REVISED ●

The word 'hijab' means a partition, barrier or screen, usually between one person and another. Commonly, it is understood to refer to modesty in dress, for both men and women.

For women, hijab is usually understood to mean a headscarf, while some also wear a face veil.

Apart from the hijab of the body, Muslims also emphasise the hijab of the eyes, heart, thought and intention. The general conduct of a person, such as the way they talk and walk, is also part of their modesty.

> **Now test yourself**
>
> 8   Give one challenge to and one defence of hijab.
>
> TESTED ◯

Some see the hijab and veil as emblems of inequality, an outdated and discriminatory practice that needs to be challenged on the basis of human freedom, and a barrier to social integration. For others, they are a statement of faith and symbol of empowerment, worn freely with pride, and also a means of protection against sexual harassment.

Suggested answer guidance to exam practice at **www.hoddereducation.co.uk/myrevisionnotesdownloads**

Is there gender equality in Islam?

For gender equality	Against gender equality
+ The Qur'an promises equal rewards to men and women for their devotion to faith	+ Men can marry non-Muslims, but women cannot
+ The Prophet Muhammad was a passionate advocate of women's rights in a patriarchal society, rejecting female infanticide and emphasising the need for girls to be educated	+ The husband is solely responsible for the family home and must share his earnings with his wife, while the wife does not have the same obligation
+ Islam provided rights to women centuries before other cultures and the West	+ There are more religious demands on men than women. Men cannot be exempt from prayer and fasting but women who are menstruating, are pregnant or have just given birth can

Research activity

Produce a Venn diagram comparing the feminist views of Professor Aisha Abd Al Rahman and Haleh Afshar.

Chapter summary

+ There are many teachings in the Qur'an about gender equality, including the spiritual rewards for men and women being the same.
+ Some practices in Muslim societies, such as clothing and FGM, have been influenced by local cultural norms and can be argued to be independent of Islam.
+ Muslim thought has been influenced by immigration into Britain and encounters with Western values and secular rights.
+ There are different contemporary attitudes in Islam about marriage, celibacy, homosexuality and transgender issues.
+ Interpretations about Surah 4: 34 and the right of women to lead prayers differ.
+ The work of feminists like Professor Aisha Abd Al Rahman and Haleh Afshar has focused on returning to the roots of Islam to highlight the rights and status of women.

Exam practice

Explore the challenge of feminism in Islam today.   [Pearson Edexcel, AO1, 8]

Assess the claim that there is not gender equality in Islam.   [OCR, AO1/AO2, 40]

'The Muslim family is central to the Islamic religion.' Evaluate this view.

[Eduqas, AO2, 30]

10 Dialogues

Qur'anic teachings on the meaning of human existence

The Qur'an teaches that the main reason for human existence is to worship God. Humans must also be in the service of God through serving his creation. They must additionally lead moral and ethical lives as they are being tested through life and death.

These teachings form the underpinning of Islamic ethics.

Adam's creation and knowledge of God

REVISED ●

Adam is believed to be the first human Allah spoke to directly. Islam teaches that everyone is born in a state of 'Islam' (submission to Allah), therefore Adam was also the first Muslim. Adam and his wife Hawwa (Eve) lived in a heavenly garden. They were forbidden from approaching a particular tree but Satan tempted them to do so. Although Adam expressed remorse, Allah banished them from the garden. The story of the creation of Adam suggests several things about humanity:

Teachings about Adam	What this may suggest about humanity
Qur'an 40: 67 teaches that Adam was created from clay, water and dust	This may be a metaphor for people's mouldable nature
Hawwa was created from Adam's rib	Some interpret this to mean that Hawwa was subservient to Adam, but others suggest that it means that she was of the same nature as him
Adam was taught many things and when angels were challenged to show their knowledge, they were unable to match him	This demonstrates humanity's intellectual capacity
Allah 'took out the offspring from the loins of the children of Adam' and asked them, 'Am I not your Lord?' (Qur'an 7: 172)	This rhetorical style of questioning suggests that all humans are born with an innate knowledge of God
Adam's sons Cain and Abel were asked to make sacrifices to Allah. Allah accepted Abel's sacrifice because of Abel's righteousness and Cain, out of jealousy, killed him	This reflects humanity's corruptible nature and need for divine teachings to enable people to behave ethically and have a relationship with Allah

Worship of God

REVISED ●

Islam has two cornerstones:
1 Huquq Allah – rights due to Allah
2 Huquq al-`Ibad – rights due to his creation.

These underpin all aspects of human behaviour. They also link to the purpose of human creation which has been made clear in the Qur'an: 'I created jinn and mankind only to worship Me.' (Qur'an 51: 56).

The Arabic word for worship 'ibadah' also refers to formal prayers such as Salah. Through acts of worship, in which they seek to connect with a higher being, believers are reminded of their shared humanity with others in the world. Muslims believe it is this attitude that inspires them to help and support other human beings who have likewise been created by Allah. This is also the reason prophets have been sent who have echoed the same teaching.

Muslims do not believe Allah is in need of worship, as he is perfect. Rather, it is human beings that require 'ibadah' to connect them with Allah and to motivate them to develop deeper connections with his creation. This links also to the role of human beings as caliphs (trustees) of the Earth (see Chapter 8). This can be expressed in multiple ways, from becoming doctors and nurses to improve people's health, to donating money to charitable causes. Fulfilling the objectives of 'ibadah' can lead to a life of peace, both in this life and the next.

Moral tribulation

REVISED

Muhammad said: 'The world is a prison-house for a believer and Paradise for a non-believer.' (Hadith – Sahih Muslim, 2956).

This suggests that, for a Muslim, staying on the right path in order to please Allah can be challenging – a greater Jihad. In contrast, a non-believer may feel that they can enjoy more freedom.

This struggle in the lives of believers, in which they may experience various tests of faith, is called a moral tribulation.

> We shall certainly test you with fear and hunger, and loss of property, lives, and crops. But [Prophet], give good news to those who are steadfast, those who say, when afflicted with a calamity, 'we belong to God and to Him we shall return.' These will be given blessings and mercy from their Lord, and it is they who are rightly guided.

(Qur'an 2: 155–7, Haleem 2008)

Muslims are taught to draw comfort from the fact that nobody has gone through more tribulations than Allah's messengers, particularly Muhammad, who achieved the greatest nearness to Allah, despite facing multiple trials throughout his life.

By maintaining faith in Allah and living in accordance with his commandments, Muslims believe they can earn similar nearness to Allah. The Qur'an also teaches that this life is only temporary and that any difficulties experienced in this life for the sake of Allah will be rewarded in the next. This is one of the ways that Muslims respond to the question of suffering.

The dialogue between Islam and ethics

REVISED

Muslims believe that every aspect of human behaviour, private and public, is recorded and judged by Allah. This shows the importance of moral conduct in Islam.

> **Exam tip**
>
> Refer back to greater Jihad (see Chapter 5) and make links with Islamic teachings about morality.

How does Islam compare with different ethical theories ?

Deontological	Islamic position
This a duty-based theory, normally associated with Immanuel Kant, who believed that morality can be known through reason. Humans are responsible for doing good to others. The rightness or wrongness of an action is determined by the action itself ('do the right thing'). Every human being has intrinsic worth	The two core fundamental principles of Islam – Huquq Allah and Huquq al-`Ibad (see page 102) underpin all other aspects of the faith including the Five Pillars (Sunni) and Ten Obligatory Acts (Shi'a) (see Chapter 5) Muslims believe in the sanctity of life and that intentions are key to actions, as taught by Muhammad

Teleological or consequentialist	Islamic position
This theory focuses on the results of an action. An example of this approach is Utilitarianism which tries to create the greatest happiness for the greatest number, as seen in the thinking of Jeremy Bentham who prioritised the pursuit of pleasure and avoidance of pain	Islam teaches that the aim is to achieve peace in society as the greatest good. Pursuing personal desires (for example, alcohol, sex) does not always lead to this, but in fact the opposite. Materialistic happiness is temporary whereas striving to be close to Allah leads to true and lasting contentment (Qur'an 13: 28, 29: 64, 40: 39 and 55: 26)

Character based (virtue ethics)	Islamic position
This is a theory about acquiring virtue through practice. It was developed by Aristotle and other ancient Greek philosophers and states that by practising things like honesty, courage and justice – at the right place and the right time, with the right intention – a person develops an honourable and moral character	Muslims believe the Qur'an and Hadith encourage lived values such as sincerity, service and sacrifice. Qualities such as justice and forgiveness only become moral when used at the appropriate time and place. For instance, forgiveness is a virtue when it helps a sinner to reform, but not when it encourages them to continue doing evil

Islamic ethics appear to be a combination of deontological, teleological/consequentialist and character-based approaches, which Muslims believe confirms its comprehensiveness as a faith.

You can find more about Islam's responses to various ethical issues throughout this book. For example:

Life and death – page 88

Animal rights – page 90

LGBT issues – page 98

Wealth – page 56

Tolerance – page 113

Freedom of religion – page 113

Free will and moral responsibility – page 46

Muslims also believe in the importance of pure conscience in decision making, and in a voice of Allah from within, which indicate the morality of a decision or action. This can be achieved when a person has become God-conscious and seeks forgiveness from wrong (Qur'an 3: 135–6).

Now test yourself

1 Is Islam a deontological, teleological/consequentialist or character based ethic theory?

TESTED ◯

The dialogue between Islam and philosophy

Historically, the relationship between Islam and philosophy has varied between harmonious and hostile. Muslims believe reason has an important place in Islam. The Qur'an contains many references to using the intellect to reflect over creation and to acquire knowledge. This was the basis for the use of ijtihad and qiyas in Islamic thought (see Chapter 3).

Suggested answer guidance to exam practice at **www.hoddereducation.co.uk/myrevisionnotesdownloads**

The Muslims involved in translating Greek works into Arabic and Persian were influenced by the ideas of Plato and Aristotle and wrote their own commentaries based on logic and rationalism. This led to a conflict between some theologians, more notably Al-Ghazali and Ibn Rushd, about enlightenment through divinely revealed truths and mysticism alone, and the use of human reason. As the leading commentator on the Greeks, Ibn Rushd's works had a major influence on later figures like St Thomas Aquinas and Moses Maimonides and were the catalyst for a reformation of both Christian and Jewish thought, introducing the concept of rationalism in religion.

> Muslims believe that there are limits to the use of reason in understanding Allah and that the furthest rational thinking can take a person is to accept the existence of Allah. However, humans have also been given spiritual faculties through which they can reach certainty that Allah exists (for example, revelation). This makes statements about faith meaningful, not just for Muslims but for anyone who has experienced God, as his existence has been verified and also informs the way they live their life (for example, performing extra prayers, becoming more charitable). Therefore, for many Muslims, the nature of faith is more a belief in Allah rather than just a belief that he is real.
>
> Muslims do not see any incoherence in their beliefs but see all sources of authority as compatible with each other, with the Qur'an as the most important (see Chapter 3).

Miracles

REVISED

There are two definitions of the word 'miracle':
+ instances of divine action that defy the laws of nature
+ rare, highly significant or inexplicable events that do not – or only seem to – violate scientific laws.

Both definitions are used by Muslims. In Islam, miracles are unique events performed by Allah or with Allah's permission. For centuries, they have contributed to establishing the truth of Allah's prophets and his own existence.

An example of a miracle is when Musa (Moses) parted the Red Sea to lead the Israelites from Egypt to Palestine to escape persecution by the Fir'awn (Pharaoh) (Qur'an 26: 60–7).

The two definitions of a miracle can apply to this event:
+ Many Muslims believe that Allah enabled Musa to perform this miracle, directly intervening against the known laws of nature.
+ Others believe Allah worked through nature to make it possible by using the ebb tide when the water receded enough to make a crossing by foot possible, but trapping the Fir'awn's army when the tide rose again.

Religious experience

REVISED

A religious experiences is when someone believes they have been in contact with God or have felt his presence. It is through religious experiences that the world's religions began, such as Musa hearing the voice of Allah and Muhammad receiving revelations of the Qur'an.

In Islam, religious experiences occur in a variety of ways including:
1 revelations and prophecies
2 miracles
3 visions and dreams
4 worship and prayers.

Religious experiences are not confined to one religion or one place: between 31 and 49 per cent of British people claim to have had direct personal awareness of 'a power or presence different from everyday life'. The numbers are similar in the USA. Muslims say that this is evidence that Allah is accessible to all, including those of no faith. For example, in relation to prayer,

Allah promises that he will respond to those who reach out to him: '[Prophet], if My servants ask you about Me, I am near. I respond to those who call Me.' (Qur'an 2: 186).

Sceptics have questioned whether religious experiences are real and have presented alternative explanations for these claims.

+ Psychology – thinkers like Sigmund Freud argued that religion and religious experiences are an illusion and the product of people's desires.
+ Physiology – some claim that those with temporal lobe epilepsy are more likely to experience hallucinations that predispose them to faith. This may have included holy figures in the past.
+ Sociology – Karl Marx explained religion as a form of social control that makes believers behave in a certain way and distracts them from reality.

Many religious people counter these by suggesting that such criticisms do not disprove or invalidate belief in God, religious experiences have been testified to by hundreds of thousands of prophets and their followers, and religious teachings promote freedom rather than suppression. Furthermore, prophets live pure lives and cannot lie about God (Qur'an 10: 16). They had no power and were persecuted, yet flourished despite this, demonstrating that they must have had divine support.

Kalam cosmological argument

REVISED ●

The cosmological argument is also known as the first cause argument and states that everything in the universe must have had a beginning. The only exception is Allah who is eternal and incomparable (Qur'an 112: 1–4).

The earliest known version of the cosmological argument is the one put forward by the Kalam philosophers, including the eleventh-century reformer Al-Ghazali. The Kalam thinkers presented a philosophical argument about Allah being the ultimate cause of everything, which states:

1 Whatever begins to exist must have a cause.
2 The universe began to exist and so must have a cause.
3 The cause of the universe must itself be uncaused.
4 The uncaused cause is Allah.

Criticisms of the cosmological argument include:

+ If God is the cause of everything, something must have caused him to exist (Bertrand Russell).
+ It does not have to be the God of the Abrahamic faiths who brought the universe into being.
+ There could have been multiple gods who were responsible for the origins of the universe.
+ We are unable to make sense of anything beyond this universe and therefore cannot justify an infinite cause (David Hume).

> **Exam tip**
>
> See page 81 for more on the Kalam cosmological argument.

Muslims respond by pointing to Allah's unique nature and his transcendence and omnipotence.

The Qur'an also rejects the idea that there are two or more omnipotent powers governing the universe. This is because:

+ it goes against the basis of Islam which is tawhid (God's oneness)
+ Allah does not require the help of anything or anyone
+ if there were multiple deities, there would be conflict between them (Qur'an 21: 22).

Teleological argument

REVISED ●

This is also known as the design argument. It is based on the belief that the order, beauty and complexity of the universe is the work of God.

The Qur'an contains many teachings encouraging humans to study and reflect on creation and provides arguments about its design.

Suggested answer guidance to exam practice at **www.hoddereducation.co.uk/myrevisionnotesdownloads**

Muslims believe that there are many 'signs' Allah has given through creation. Humans have been given intelligence and the ability to use reason to understand that a well-ordered and balanced world could not have been the product of chance.

Critics of the teleological argument, like David Hume, argued that the world is 'very faulty and imperfect' and also point to the presence of suffering as evidence of poor design.

However, Muslims believe that suffering plays an important part in all aspects of life as a:
+ test of faith or patience
+ warning or punishment from God
+ source of developing qualities such as strength and resilience
+ way of appreciating happiness and goodness
+ consequence of free will and actions
+ means of helping others.

It is also essential for evolution, without which life itself would stop advancing. Therefore, suffering forms part of a perfect design, with the good and the bad, as it helps to fulfil God's purpose for humans (Qur'an 3: 190–1).

The Islamic Golden Age

The Islamic Golden Age (see Chapter 7) was a period of great progress in science, but also saw important advancements in philosophical thought. The Translation Movement translated ancient Greek works on philosophy, maths and medicine into Arabic. The Abbasids paid translators huge salaries, reflecting the importance of knowledge of these fields at this time. This was alongside the ongoing development of understanding the Qur'an and other sources of Islamic law.

Two key scholars of this period were Al-Ghazali and Ibn Rushd (known in the West as Averroes). They built on the learning inherited from the Greeks but drew different conclusions about the compatibility between philosophical thinking and Islam.

Al-Ghazali 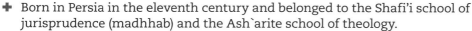 REVISED

+ Born in Persia in the eleventh century and belonged to the Shafi'i school of jurisprudence (madhhab) and the Ash`arite school of theology.
+ Wrote extensively on Sunni thought and law.
+ Called Hujjat al-Islam (the Proof of Islam) due to the wisdom of his writings and his devout life.

Ibn Rushd REVISED

+ A Spanish doctor, astronomer, philosopher and judge.
+ Inspired by Aristotle and influenced St Thomas, who called him 'the Commentator' due to his commentaries on Aristotle.
+ Despite the Ash`arite ban on philosophy, his work was a key inspiration for the European Renaissance.

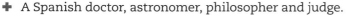

Al-Ghazali	Ibn Rushd
+ Al-Ghazali rejected a lot of the Greek ideas that he felt had infiltrated Muslim thought, believing that that philosophy (which promotes questioning) had no place in the study of Islam in which divine commandments are beyond scrutiny + His *The Incoherence of the Philosophers* was a criticism of the falsafa (intellectuals) such as Ibn Sina (known in the West as Avicenna) who were inspired by Greek writings	+ Ibn Rushd was greatly influenced by Aristotle and argued that philosophy should have a recognised status in Islam. He said that philosophy and revelation are different means of reaching the same truth, though it is for experts to practise philosophy. He said the Qur'an encourages philosophical thought + He argued that the scientific method and philosophy empower individuals to better understand the Qur'an and therefore Allah

A-level Religious Studies: Islam

Al-Ghazali	Ibn Rushd
<ul><li>Al-Ghazali identified twenty doctrinal errors that he believed philosophers had made, three of which he said were heretical:<ul><li>The world is eternal – this clashes with the belief that only Allah is without cause</li><li>Allah knows generalities but not particulars – contradicts belief in divine omniscience</li><li>There is no bodily resurrection – contradicts traditional understandings about life after death</li></ul></li><li>He also criticised Ibn Sina's view that Allah must act in particular ways. This undermined the Ash`arite position on Allah's omnipotence, which states he is not bound by any laws (thus can cause miracles) and causes all things to happen (occasionalism)</li></ul>	<ul><li>He pointed to difficulties with understanding revealed texts, such as the Injil and the Qur'an, without employing rational thought</li><li>He responded to Al-Ghazali's attack with his book *The Incoherence of the Incoherence* in which he refuted each argument and explained three levels of religious knowledge (rhetorical, dialectical and demonstrative)</li><li>Ibn Rushd agreed with much of Al-Ghazali's criticisms of Ibn Sina but only because it was a distortion of Aristotelian thought, therefore Al-Ghazali's criticism of Aristotle was misplaced</li><li>For Ibn Rushd, Al-Ghazali's critique itself demonstrated traits of philosophical reasoning that he was defending</li></ul>

Al-Ghazali's two crises and salvation

REVISED

In *al-Munqidh min al-Dalal* (*Deliverance from Error*), Al-Ghazali refers to two crises. The first was when he experienced a period of epistemological scepticism (doubt about what is knowable) before being saved by 'a light which God most high cast into my breast'.

The second occurred during his time as Professor of Theology at the University of Baghdad. He had devoted a lot of his time to writing about the big philosophical and theological questions, including trying to prove the existence of God through rational thinking. However, he was never satisfied with his own arguments and struggled to reconcile rationality with spirituality. This caused a breakdown while he was giving a lecture – he became unable to speak, something he attributed to God. He left his job and family to live a life of piety, convinced that the way to truth was the path of the prophets: moving away from a self-centred life to one that was focused purely on Allah. He became more minimalistic and sought nearness to Allah through Sufi practices. This, he believed, leads to a proper understanding of scripture.

He also went to Makkah for pilgrimage. It was around this time that he was recognised as the mujaddid, a reformer in Islam that Muhammad said would appear in each century (Hadith – Abu Dawud). The scholar Taqi Al-Din Al-Subki said that Al-Ghazali was the closest person to prophethood after the Prophet Muhammad.

Upon returning to Iran, Al-Ghazali lived a humble life and taught about the superiority of Sufi knowledge over intellectual searches for God. He became convinced that while the heart can experience direct confirmation of union with Allah, reason cannot. This did not stop him employing philosophical reasoning, as he continued to present his Kalam cosmological argument for the existence of Allah when the need arose for academic purposes. The ideas of Al-Ghazali continue to have a significant impact in the Muslim world.

Now test yourself

2 What was the main disagreement between Al-Ghazali and Ibn Rushd?

TESTED

Exam practice

'Muslim ethics can be considered to be deontological.' Evaluate this claim. [AQA, AO2, 15]

To what extent was Ibn Rushd's argument for the necessity of philosophy according to the shari`a convincing?

[OCR, AO1/AO2, 40]

Chapter summary

+ The worship of God and service to his creation underpin philosophical and ethical approaches in Islam.
+ Muslim ethics combine deontological, teleological/consequentialist and character-based theories as an indication of the comprehensiveness of Islam.
+ The value of philosophy was debated by Al-Ghazali and Ibn Rushd who drew different conclusions about its compatibility with Islam.

Suggested answer guidance to exam practice at **www.hoddereducation.co.uk/myrevisionnotesdownloads**

11 State, society and secularisation

Madinah as the model state

Muslims believe that the ideal state was established by the Prophet Muhammad in Madinah following the hijrah in 622CE. This was because it was governed according to shari`a principles as documented in the Constitution of Madinah, which covered religious, social, moral and political matters, and laid down how people of different faiths should coexist.

Exam tip

You can find more about The Constitution of Madinah on page 18.

Religious structure

Muhammad's mosque (see page 54) became the centre of the teaching, practice and preaching of Islam. It was here that Muhammad would lead prayers, hold meetings and engage in dialogue with Jews and Christians. It was also here that the qiblah changed from Jerusalem to Madinah (Qur'an 2: 144–50) and freedom of belief was guaranteed to all.

> There is no compulsion in religion.

(Qur'an 2: 256, Haleem 2008)

Moral structure

The Constitution promoted a new code of ethics that encouraged mutual respect between all the communities of Madinah. This applied within the economic context of the time with the redistribution of wealth from Zakah, a new culture of honest trade and the prohibition of charging interest on loans to prevent exploitation of those in need.

> God has allowed trade and forbidden usury.

(Qur'an 2: 276, Haleem 2008)

Social structure

Muhammad set up a system between the Muhajirun or migrants (from Makkah) and Ansar or helpers (converts in Madinah) whereby each helper took in a migrant and treated them like a family member. This set a precedent for the treatment and integration of asylum seekers.

> Those who were already firmly established in their homes (in Medina), and firmly rooted in faith, show love for those who migrated to them for refuge and harbour no resentment in their hearts for what has been given to them. They give them preference over themselves, even if they too are poor.

(Qur'an 59: 9, Haleem 2008)

The term 'ummah' was originally used for all citizens of Madinah, including non-Muslims, before it changed to mean the worldwide body of Muslims. Muhammad appointed the Ethiopian slave Bilal ibn Rabah to be the first Muslim to make the call to prayer, and also upheld the rights of women (see Chapter 9), thus promoting racial and gender equality.

Political structure

The tribal chiefs of Madinah unanimously appointed Muhammad as their leader as they believed that his skills and qualities made him ideal to take charge of city. He was able to organise a state, not in the modern sense of the term (as tribes still existed), but one that sought to provide rights and protection to all citizens on the condition that they all followed the same rules and did not break tribal alliances. However, it is still considered to have been closer to a modern secular pluralist government than a theocracy. Muhammad was able to reconcile and make peace between conflicting tribes, even when hostilities had reached boiling point.

Muhammad also became the military commander for Muslims when they were forced to fight in self-defence (Chapters 2 and 5).

There were times when Muhammad punished those who worked against Islam and violated the terms of the Constitution. Some of these were expelled from Madinah (e.g. Banu Nadir), while others were sentenced to death, such as Ka'b ibn Ashraf and members of the Banu Qurayzah. This was justified under the law of qisas (see Chapter 8).

Now test yourself
TESTED ◯

1 Write down two ways in which Madinah was seen as a model state.

Religion and state in pre-modern Islam
REVISED ◯

In the Sunni tradition:
+ The Caliph (Khalifah) is the guardian of Islamic law. The four Rightly Guided Caliphs had both spiritual and temporal authority, continuing from the role of Muhammad.
+ Each Caliph was appointed with the agreement of the community and would consult a shura (consultative body), pointing to the contractual nature of their role. Muftis were also appointed with the authority to pass edicts (fatwas). There were times when the Caliph changed his mind, following the advice of other believers. The ummah was a brotherhood of believers based on religious rather than tribal solidarity.
+ The role of the Caliphs was to consolidate Islam, defend and expand Muslim borders and uphold shari'a.
+ The collapse of the Rightly Guided Caliphate following Ali's assassination led to the rule of the Umayyad and Abbasid dynasties (see Chapter 6). The Abbasid Caliphs sometimes came into conflict with the ulama (religious scholars) and so ruled separately from them. The rulers often controlled many political affairs (managing the government and the army, and providing services) whereas religious officials handled religious and family matters. This continues to be the case in many Muslim countries.

In the Shi'a tradition:
+ The Imam has supreme authority, and is considered to be perfect, pure and infallible.
+ Each of the twelve Imams were from the ahl al-bayt and were chosen by the preceding Imam (nass) and given responsibility for guiding people on the correct understanding of the Qur'an. This makes them the best of humanity (afdal al-nas).
+ In the absence of the twelfth Imam Muhammad Al-Mahdi (who is believed to be in hiding), Shi'a Muslims who belong to the Twelver tradition (see page 43) seek guidance from the Marja' Taqlid (Grand Ayatollahs) who are the highest authorities in Shi'a jurisprudence and most senior among the ulama. When the Mahdi comes, he will be the final authority.

State and religion were historically closely associated in both Sunni and Shi'a communities. Some say Sunni Islam was defined and sharpened in the face of challenges of sectarianism and the alternative political model introduced by Shi'a Muslims.

Now test yourself
TESTED ◯

2 Give two similarities and two differences between Sunni and Shi'a attitudes about the relationship between religion and the state.

Suggested answer guidance to exam practice at **www.hoddereducation.co.uk/myrevisionnotesdownloads**

Shari`a law within a Muslim state

Muslim states governed according to shari`a principles place Allah at the centre of everything, informing the religious, political, social and economic life of society (see Chapter 3). To this end, the religious qualities of political leaders are considered extremely important. For example, in Iran, representatives must be vetted and confirmed to be pious and to belong to the ahl al-bayt before being given office. In many Muslim countries, heads of state will also recite the Shahadah and other Islamic declarations when being sworn into office.

There is no uniformity across the Muslim world regarding the understanding and implementation of Islamic law.

Iran	The laws of a parliament, known as Majlis, must be authorised by religious leaders as compliant with shari`a. Women can serve in the government and in 1997 Masoumeh Ebtekar became the first female vice-president
Saudi Arabia	The country is a monarchy ruled by the House of Saud family and follows Islamic law. They follow the Salafi strand of Islam which advocates a return to the original Islam of Muhammad, independent of schools of thought
Pakistan	A former British colony, Pakistan retains British law as its main system of law and has Islam as the state religion. Shari`a law courts adjudicate on religious and family matters though these can be overruled by a higher secular court
Turkey	Ottoman rule paved the way for a modern, secular state in which some social policies (for example, legalisation of homosexuality) were implemented many years before they were implemented in the UK. President Mustafa Ataturk's reforms in the early twentieth century allowed Muslims to practise their faith freely under secular principles, without the state imposing any religious rules

The early Islamic caliphate is often looked on as an ideal by many Muslims who wish to return to the ways of Muhammad and his successors. This has motivated groups like Hizb ut-Tahrir to call for bringing back the caliphate, while Ahmadiyya Muslims claim that they have a caliphate based on the teachings of the Qur'an and Hadith.

Varying views of shari`a law within a non-Muslim state

Some feel that fulfilling an Islamic way of life in a non-Muslim state presents great challenges to fulfilling an Islamic way of life:

1   Traditional Islamic governance has politics and religion heavily intertwined; secular societies make a point of separating the two and making religion a strictly personal matter. Democracy represents the will of humans which may not be the same as the will of Allah.

2   Secular societies may pass laws that conflict with the beliefs and morals of some Muslims or the laws of Islam given in the Qur'an. In France, some traditional Muslim dress for women has been banned. Some feel that the shifting picture of what behaviour is legal and acceptable in secular societies, like extra-marital sex or the availability of some intoxicating drugs, indicates a moral decline.

3   Living in a pluralistic society can make it harder to observe Muslim practices like Id and to follow a Muslim way of life. For example, Muslim views of modest dress may clash with the views of the wider population, resulting in stigmatisation and discrimination.

4   Secular states often allow criticism of Islam (and religion generally) in a way which would not be permitted in a Muslim society.

5   Some may feel that political secularism is a way for non-Muslim countries to control or exert pressure on Muslim countries. Countries with imperialistic intent could use secularlism as a tool to threaten sanctions and embargoes against countries that use shar`ia.

Others say that shari`a is perfectly compatible with secular and democratic values:

1   Muhammad and the Rightly Guided Caliphs established a society which included non-Muslim people, and instructed some Muslims to live in non-Muslim majority countries (for example, the first hijrah to Abyssinia), suggesting that a country with Islamic governance was not a requirement for practising Islam.

2   Secular states often ensure freedom of religion and religious practice to Muslims, even as a minority of the population. They also generally allow people of all faiths to participate in the democratic political process, including running for office. Arbitration courts, legal in the UK and many secular states, allow for Muslims to choose to have personal disputes resolved on the basis of shari`a.

3   Many Muslims feel that their beliefs are a personal matter and that most principles of modern and secular government are appropriate and compatible with Islam. They may also believe that historical ideas of justice (like capital punishment) are no longer acceptable. Additionally, many Muslim states have committed to secular codes of ethics like the Universal Declaration of Human Rights.

Islam does not advocate a specific form of government. Islam allows us absolute freedom to organise government according to the ideas, social and economic conditions of the times.

(Ali Abd'al Raziq)

The experience of non-Muslim societies can also be very different. Some democracies, like Britain, use public money to fund religious institutions and causes (for example, faith schools, religious charities), while other states, like France, ban religion from public life and state-run institutions, for instance, banning religious symbols in schools.

As there is no version of shari`a agreed by all Muslims, the diversity of interpretation informs how Muslims understand the compatibility of Islam with democracy and secularism.

> **Revision activity**
>
> Create a table providing three of the strongest arguments for and against the statement 'Islam is compatible with democracy and secularism'.

Islam and society

REVISED ●

There are two main positions in Islam in relation to the validity of other faiths. These are:

+ exclusivism: Islam is the only true faith or path
+ inclusivism: there is truth and value in faiths and paths other than Islam.

Islamic exclusivism	Islamic inclusivism
+ Allah says he has chosen Islam as the religion for humanity (Qur'an 5: 3, 3: 19) which will have victory over all faiths (Qur'an 61: 9)	+ Some from the People of the Book (ahl al-kitab), primarily monotheistic Jews and Christians, are praised for their devotion and humility (Qur'an 3: 199), the quality of their worship and acts of virtue which will be rewarded (Qur'an 3: 113–15)
+ No other religion will be acceptable to Allah 'If anyone seeks a religion other than [Islam] complete devotion to God, it will not be accepted from him: he will be one of the losers in the Hereafter.' (Qur'an 3: 85)	+ Muslims are permitted to eat the food and marry women of the People of the Book (Qur'an 5: 5)
+ Previous religions and holy books contained errors and needed to be superceded with a perfect message (Qur'an 2: 106)	+ Muhammad was instructed by Allah to confirm the truth of previous revelations and not to make any distinction between the messengers (Qur'an 2: 136)
+ Muhammad was the promised prophet in the Bible and other texts, and it is essential to believe in him	+ Faiths established previously share similar features with Islam
+ Other religions are guilty of shirk, such as Christianity which teaches about the Trinity (Qur'an 4: 171). Shirk is unforgivable (Qur'an 4: 116)	*He has laid down you for [people] the same commandment that He gave Noah, which We have revealed to you [Muhammad] and which We enjoined on Abraham and Moses and Jesus 'Uphold the faith and do not divide into factions within it' – what you (Prophet) call upon the idolaters to do is hard for them; God chooses whoever He pleases for Himself and guides towards Himself those who turn to Him.*
+ Those who don't believe that they will meet God, such as atheists, are 'lost' (Qur'an 6: 31)	(Qur'an 42: 13, Haleem 2008)

Suggested answer guidance to exam practice at **www.hoddereducation.co.uk/myrevisionnotesdownloads**

The interpretation of passages like Qur'an 3: 85 depends on whether the word 'Islam' is read as a noun or a verb:

	Islam
Noun	Religion brought by Muhammad
Meaning	'If anyone seeks a religion other than [Islam] complete devotion to God, it will not be accepted from him: he will be one of the losers in the Hereafter.' (Qur'an 3: 85) This means that only believers in Islam will go to heaven
Verb	Submitting to God
Meaning	'If anyone seeks a religion other than [Islam] complete devotion to God, it will not be accepted from him: he will be one of the losers in the Hereafter.' (Qur'an 3: 85) This means that the key to gaining a good afterlife is to submit to God. This applies to other monotheistic faiths as well and not only followers of Muhammad

The People of the Book

In the time of Muhammad, People of the Book (ahl al-kitab) was used to refer to monotheistic Jews and Christians following a previous divinely revealed message. The Qur'an mentions the People of the Book frequently to reinforce the shared heritage of the Abrahamic faiths, deriving from the same source (Allah). This is why Muslims are allowed to eat the food of and marry women from the People of the Book. People of the Book had special legal status as dhimmis under Islamic rule (see page 116).

Pluralism

Muslims believe that Muhammad was a messenger not just for Muslims, but the entire world (Qur'an 7: 158). Religious differences with those of other beliefs did not stop him showing tolerance, respect and love towards them. This is the example Muslims have tried to follow ever since, with varying degrees of success.

Islam's attitude towards non-Muslims can be divided into three areas:
1 Freedom of thought and belief for all
2 Respect and regard for the beliefs and sentiments of others
3 Protection of the rights of all belief systems.

1 Freedom of thought and belief for all

+ Muhammad was given the task of restoring tawhid by inviting people to Allah, but he was merely a warner (Qur'an 88: 21–2; 42: 49).
+ Surah Al-Baqarah states, 'There is no compulsion in religion' (Qur'an 2: 256). This teaching has been understood by some groups (for example, Jama'at-e-Islami) to mean that if someone converts to Islam through their own free choice, they must remain believers. This is the basis for apostasy laws in some Muslims countries.
+ This interpretation is rejected by other Muslims who say it is inconsistent with other teachings that permit people to join and leave Islam without restriction (Qur'an 4: 137). It is also said in Surah Al-Kafiroon, 'you have your religion and I have mine' (Qur'an 109: 6).

A-level Religious Studies: Islam

2 Respect and regard for the beliefs and sentiments of others

+ Islam promotes respect for the beliefs of people of other faiths. This was exemplified by Muhammad when he reprimanded a Muslim for offending a Jew by undermining the status of Musa (Hadith – Bukhari). Additionally, a funeral procession passed in front of Muhammad and he stood up. When he was told that it was a Jewish funeral, he said, 'is he not a person?' (Hadith – Bukhari)
+ The Qur'an teaches Muslims not to 'Revile' the gods of idolators (Qur'an 6: 108), despite shirk being the worst sin in Islam.
+ Following the example of the Prophet Muhammad of showing others sympathy, Mirza Masroor Ahmad, the leader of Ahmadiyya Muslims, sent a letter to the Queen to express condolences at the passing of Prince Philip.

3 Protection of the rights of all belief systems

+ The Qur'an upholds the rights of other religions and instructs Muslims to protect their places of worship. Safeguarding freedom of belief is not just for Muslims, but all humans, and holy buildings such as churches and synagogues should be defended from possible attack (Qur'an 22: 40) (see Chapter 5).
+ Muhammad signed the 'Charter of Privileges', a promise to Christians on behalf of Muslims that they would safeguard their churches until the Day of Judgement. A copy of this historic document is still on display at St Catherine's monastery in Egypt. This protection was not honoured by ISIS terrorists who attacked the monastery in 2017 and also vowed to kill more Christians in the country.
+ On his return to Makkah, Muhammad ordered that the hundreds of idols housed in the Ka`bah be cleared. Some Muslims have interpreted this to mean that once they have authority, they have permission to do the same with buildings and landmarks honouring other gods and figures. This is cited as a reason why the Taliban destroyed two ancient Buddha statues in Afghanistan in 2001. Other Muslims say the Prophet's actions were specific to the Ka`bah, to restore it for the purpose of tawhid for which it was originally built.

> **Revision activity**
>
> Create a mind-map showing Islam's attitude to other faiths, including the headings: exclusivism, inclusivism and pluralism.

> **Now test yourself** TESTED ⬤
>
> 3 Give one example of Muslim teachings about:
> a) Freedom of thought and belief for all
> b) Respect and regard for the beliefs and sentiments of others
> c) Protection of the rights of all belief systems.

Conversion

REVISED ⬤

An important duty of Muslims is to bring people into Islam. The Qur'an teaches them to perform da'wah, meaning to invite others to the right path with 'wisdom and good teaching. Argue with them in the most courteous way' (Qur'an 16: 125). Muhammad wrote letters to neighbouring heads of state inviting them to Islam and said to Ali that 'if one man is guided on the right path (converted to Islam) through you, it would be better for you than (a great number of) red camels' (Hadith – Bukhari). (Red camels were a valuable commodity in seventh-century Arabia.)

These teachings continue to inspire many Muslims to preach in their localities, for example, by leaflets and holding book stalls on high streets in towns and city centres, and also through the use of social media.

A minority of Muslims see the world as divided into:
1 Dar al-Islam (abode of Islam) – Muslim state
2 Dar al-harb (abode of war) – non-Muslim state.

Suggested answer guidance to exam practice at **www.hoddereducation.co.uk/myrevisionnotesdownloads**

Their aim is to convert as many people as possible in order to expand Dar al-Islam and to re-establish the caliphate. However, the overwhelming majority of Muslims believe that forced conversions are forbidden and if someone is not persuaded by Islam, they should be left in peace (Qur'an 43: 88–89).

Some question the coherence in approaches to conversion in Islam. Some Muslim men who marry Christian or Jewish women do not require them to convert, and there are also Muslims who refer to a person's embracing of Islam as 'reversion', as a reference to their return to their natural born state of being a Muslim.

Justice and liberation

REVISED

+ Justice, liberation and mercy lie at the heart of Islam. Muslims believe this is why Islam was revealed at a time when social inequalities were rife during the days of Jahiliyya.
+ The Qur'an and Sunnah provide guidance on the need to support the poor and defend the oppressed, both to preserve individual rights and to serve the public interest (maslahah). This is contained in the communal responsibility (fard kifayah) for Muslims to promote good and forbid wrong (al-Amr bil-Ma'ruf wa al-Nahy `anil-Munkar).
+ Justice and liberation have links to Zakah (alms giving), greater Jihad (the inner struggle to support Islam, within an individual believer's faith) and lesser Jihad (the outward struggle through social or military efforts) (see Chapter 5).
+ Some Muslims believe liberation has implications for applying regulations to control the social order in order to preserve the fundamental rights of all members of society.

> **Liberation** The state of freedom from any type of oppression or limit on thought and expression. In Islam 'liberation' relates to challenging injustice and bringing about social reform

There are different contemporary approaches and attitudes to social liberation in Islam which affect the way many Muslims live out their faith. Some, like Ali Shari'ati, advocated the need for practical action to resist oppression, while others, such as Abdal Hakim Murad, call for individual purification in order to effect wider change.

Ali Shari'ati (1933–77)

REVISED

+ Shari'ati said that historically all prophets stood up to injustice to free the oppressed. This was also exemplified by Muhammad's companions such as Abu Dharr who, according to Shari'ati, denounced the Sunni caliphs as corrupt, and Yazid to whom Imam Hussain refused to pay allegiance.
+ Shari'ati was influenced by Marxist (socialist) ideas and is seen as the inspiration for the Iranian revolution (1979) that toppled the US-backed Shah. He advocated social revolution that would end all forms of exploitation, eradicate poverty and capitalism, modernise the economy, and ultimately establish a just, dynamic and classless society.
+ He was very critical of the apolitical Shi'ism of the Iranian elite. Shi'ism, to him, was a revolutionary ideology that permeated all spheres of life, including politics. Muhammad came to establish not just a religious community but an ummah in continuous movement towards progress and social justice.
+ Shari'ati's ideas were not supported by religious leaders who advised followers to focus on individual devotion and not to pre-empt God's plan for the world by involvement in politics.

Abdal Hakim Murad (1960–)

REVISED

+ Murad adopts a traditionalist Sufi approach and calls for a return to 'activism within'.
+ He is critical of Islamist revivalism as much of it lays the blame for Muslim problems on the West, rather than focusing on individual spiritual renewal as was the practice of the early Muslims.

+ Murad believes in the importance of the pursuit of a sound heart (qalb salim), without which nothing will be of use on the Day of Judgement (Qur'an 26: 89).

Today, many Muslim individuals and groups are actively engaged in promoting social justice through peaceful campaigning: calling upon various world political and religious leaders, urging them to establish absolute justice, create economic equity, eradicate poverty and instil service to humanity in their own nations as well as throughout the world.

Following the killing of George Floyd in Minneapolis, USA, in 2020, many Muslim MPs and organisations expressed their support for the Black Lives Matter movement and pledged their commitment to work against racism, including within their own communities.

Revision activity

Summarise the views of Ali Shari'ati and Abdul Hakim Murad in no more than 50 words each.

Non-Muslims in Muslim societies

Dhimmis

REVISED

As Islam expanded, non-Muslims living under Islamic rule were known as dhimmis. They were given rights and protection (freedom to practise their faith) in exchange for a tax payment called jizya. In Arabia this only applied to the People of the Book who were willing to live as loyal and peaceful subjects. In order to preserve tawhid in Arabia, dhimmi status was not extended to people the Muslims regarded as idolators. Jizya was not always imposed; for example, those who entered into trade agreements with Muslims could be exempt.

Dhimmis Non-Muslims living in Muslim lands

Muhammad gave strict orders for Muslims to treat dhimmis well:

> Beware, if anyone wrongs a contracting man (dhimmi), or diminishes his right, or forces him to work beyond his capacity, or takes from him anything without his consent, I shall plead for him on the Day of Judgement.

(Hadith – Abu Daud)

After Muhammad's death, jizya was levied on non-Muslims in lieu of military service. In Umar's time as Caliph, this was changed so that anyone who performed military service became exempt from paying the tax. Women, children, the elderly, the poor, people with disabilities and religious leaders were among those exempted from jizya. As part of the newly established welfare state, poor Christians and Jews were also provided with financial support from the treasury, largely through Zakah which was a heavier tax on Muslims than jizya was for dhimmis.

If Muslim authorities were unable to defend the dhimmis militarily, such as in the event of an attack by an external aggressor, they were required to return the jizya. Before he died, Umar instructed his would-be successor to take care of the dhimmis under his protection.

With the expansion of the Islamic empire, Muslims encountered other religious groups and so dhimmi status was extended to the Zoroastrians of Persia and later to Indian Hindus, Jains and Buddhists. From the eighth century, under the Umayyads, attitudes towards non-Muslims became less tolerant and the rate of jizya was sometimes increased, as a marker of the dhimmis' inferior socio-legal status.

The jizya is not collected in modern Muslim nation-states. Many, like Turkey, Algeria and Egypt, have separated religion and state and therefore grant protection and rights based on citizenship, rather than faith. Muslim scholars from more than 120 countries signed the Marrakesh Declaration (2016) which called for a new Islamic jurisprudence based on modern nation-based notions of citizenship.

Now test yourself

4 Write down two benefits of dhimmi status under a Muslim state.

TESTED

Suggested answer guidance to exam practice at **www.hoddereducation.co.uk/myrevisionnotesdownloads**

Apostasy

Apostasy is renouncing one's religion. Al-Ghazali's *Faysal al-tafriqa (On the Boundaries of Theological Tolerance in Islam)* defines apostasy in Islam as a Muslim actively rejecting key beliefs such as monotheism, Muhammad's prophethood and the afterlife.

In the Hadith, Muhammad is quoted as saying that anyone who is 'the deserter of his Din (Islam), abandoning the community' should be killed (Hadith – Muslim 16: 4152). Many Muslims cite this and other Hadiths, to justify the death penalty for apostasy. There are thirteen Muslim countries that carry the death penalty for apostasy.

In recent times, a different view has developed. It is argued that apostates who were put to death in Muhammad's time were from an earlier part of his prophethood when he followed Old Testament laws. Proponents of this view point out that the Qu'ran does not sanction the death penalty for apostates in the Qur'an. Rather, it guarantees freedom of belief (Qur'an 18: 29), including for people who keep changing their minds (Qur'an 4: 137), which, if the punishment was death, would not be possible. Muhammad was told he had no authority over anyone's beliefs (Qur'an 42: 48). The advocates of this contemporary view also say that if there is any conflict between the Qur'an and Hadith, the Qur'an must come first as it is the word of Allah and Muhammad could not say anything contrary to it (Qur'an 10: 15).

Now test yourself
TESTED

5 Provide at least one argument for and one argument against the belief that apostasy in Islam is punishable by death.

Whether throughout history or in the present time, Muslim attitudes to and treatment of other faiths and minority groups in Muslim societies have varied. When Muslims ruled Spain for 800 years between 711 and 1492CE Muslims, Jews and Christians lived in peace and harmony (this period is known as *La Convivencia*, or the Coexistence). Collectively they made significant advancements in art, architecture, literature and science. These contributions created a foundation for the Renaissance and Enlightenment of Europe. Jews and Christians who lived in Muslim Spain enjoyed more freedoms and protection than their co-religionists in other parts of Europe; some non-Muslims also migrated to Spain for this reason. When India was ruled by the Mughals, they helped to build Hindu temples and also oversaw the maintenance of Hindu pilgrimage centres such as Ayodhya, Mathura and Vrindavan.

Attitudes elsewhere have not been so tolerant. Under the Ottoman Empire, non-Muslims were not considered equal to Muslims. They had to pay special taxes and were prohibited from bearing arms, riding horses and testifying against Muslims in court. They were called 'gavours' (infidels) and could not build places of worship. In the time of the Abbasids, refusal to pay jizya could be punished with death, while under the Mamluk sultanate in fourteenth-century Egypt, dhimmis were humiliated, had signs put on their houses and were forced to wear coloured turbans. This is said to have led to many dhimmis converting to Islam in order to escape this mistreatment.

Christians and Ahmadiyya Muslims continue to experience persecution, especially in the Middle East, Pakistan and North Africa. They are denied many rights such as freedom of belief. This is despite many of these countries signing up to the Universal Declaration of Human Rights. The Marrakesh Declaration (2016) saw Muslim scholars from more than 120 countries commit themselves to the principles of the Constitution of Madinah to uphold the rights of religious minorities and for Muslims to develop inclusive ideas of citizenship.

Muslims in non-Muslim societies

Migration and identity

REVISED ●

Ever since the time of Muhammad, Muslims have migrated for religious, political and economic reasons (see Chapters 2 and 5). The first large group of Muslims arrived in Britain in the eighteenth century. They were sailors employed by the East India Company, so the first Muslim communities were established in port towns. Over time, more Muslims arrived and established a growing presence in different parts of the UK.

In the 1950s, the British government encouraged migrants from the Commonwealth to come to the UK to rebuild the country after the Second World War. Many of those who came from countries like India and Pakistan were Muslim. The arrival and growth of many diverse communities made Britain multicultural. In more recent times, discrimination and conflict in countries like Syria has led to a mass migration of Muslims looking for safety in Europe. In 2018, Office for National Statistics figures put the number of Muslims in Britain at 3.4 million (5.1 per cent of the population). That figure has risen since. There are projections that by 2050, around 40 per cent of Britons will be from migrant backgrounds.

Challenges faced by migrants

REVISED ●

British Muslims come from many different countries and sects. Many have integrated into life in Britain and embraced British values of democracy, the rule of law, individual liberty, mutual respect and tolerance for those of other faiths and beliefs. Many have become highly successful. However, there are also challenges:

+ Some of the early Muslim migrants were well educated, including those with PhDs, but struggled to get jobs that they were qualified for.
+ Early migrants experienced racism, made worse by Enoch Powell's 'River of Blood' speech in 1968 in reaction to the arrival of South Asians from East Africa.
+ In some areas of the UK, there are large concentrations of Muslims who prefer to remain segregated from the rest of society. Potential causes include:
  + significant sections of the Muslim community are less aspirational and therefore less wealthy, resulting in them living or staying in neighbourhoods with fewer opportunities
  + conservative interpretations of Islam have led some to avoid mixing with non-Muslims.
+ This segregation has led to issues like overcrowded housing, low levels of parental engagement with mainstream schools and academic achievement, and anti-Muslim prejudice.
+ Many terrorists who have acted in the name of Islam were integrated members of society and chose to adopt extremist beliefs.
+ An expectation not only to integrate (for example, contributing to the economy) but also to assimilate (for example, socialising with others, such as in pubs) has made many Muslims feel uncomfortable about compromising on their beliefs and values.

Now test yourself TESTED ●

6 Identify two challenges Muslims have faced when settling in the UK.

Food

The Qur'an stipulates that Muslims must eat halal meat, but this is not always available. Meat in supermarkets and restaurants is not always slaughtered according to halal principles or clearly labelled to indicate whether it is halal. Halal options are provided in many official settings, like schools, which helps Muslims to feel respected in British society.

Alcohol

Muslims consider alcohol to be haram. This has led to challenges with networking, company socials and career advancement, as some Muslims choose to avoid any place where alcohol is served. Others do not mind this socialising, as long as they do not drink themselves, and some Muslim shopkeepers and restaurateurs are happy to sell and serve alcohol.

Dress

The Qur'an requires both men and women to dress modestly as part of their hijab (see Chapter 9). Women's dress, such as the veil, has been a focus of attention and seen to be a hindrance to communication and obstacle to integration. In response, it is argued that any form of dress based on personal preference and religious practice is part of individual liberty, a core British value, which should not be interfered with. Additionally, the hijab has not stopped some women from playing a full and active part in society and progressing to senior roles in public life. For example, Fatima Manji was Britain's first hijab-wearing TV newsreader in 2016.

Diversity of Muslim belief

The UK's secular society facilitates a great diversity of thought and religious practice among British Muslims which might not be seen in Muslim countries. For example:
+ some groups, like Barelwi Muslims, celebrate Muhammad's birthday (Mawlid, also known as Milad al-Nabi) with processions, while others, like Deobandi Muslims, prohibit celebration of the occasion
+ different denominations celebrate Id on different days as some rely on moon sightings in the UK while others go with sightings in the nearest or their native Muslim countries.

The freedom enjoyed by Muslims in the UK has facilitated extremely liberal forms of practices (for example, Amina Wadud, who leads mixed prayers – see Chapter 9) as well as the more extremist beliefs that led to some imams being banned from entering the country. A survey conducted by Ipsos MORI in 2018 highlighted the wide range of attitudes among Muslims in response to questions about identity, belonging and terrorism. This diversity of thought and practice is not widely understood by the UK's non-Muslim majority, who tend to view Muslims as a homogenous group; often the most extreme or segregated Muslims are taken to represent the whole.

Religious practice

Many Muslims attend daily and Friday prayers frequently, some taking time off work specially to meet these commitments. The observance of Ramadan can pose challenges in a non-Muslim country where only a small percentage of the population is fasting. This can become more difficult in the summer months when fasts can last up to around eighteen hours.

Education

Muslims give importance to both religious and secular learning. In addition to attending school in the day, many Muslim children attend madrasahs in the evening and at weekends for classes in Qur'an and Arabic, and lessons on other aspects of Islam. Some madrasahs have been exposed for promotion of extremism and the use of corporal punishment. Many parents prefer sending their children to faith-based schools because of their emphasis on religious values and focus on spiritual as well as academic development, and the government allows these schools to operate legally. The 'Trojan Horse' controversy in 2014 raised concerns about some state schools being used to promote traditional Muslim beliefs and practices (for example, separation of boys and girls). There have also been challenges with parts of the curriculum, such as swimming in public pools, dance lessons and sex education.

Can Muslims integrate into a secular and European society?

REVISED

Yes	No
+ Many Muslims have succeeded in preserving their Muslim identity while pursuing successful careers in business, politics and other professions	+ Some Muslims fear losing their identity through assimilating. They feel that to maintain the purity of their traditions, such as praying five times a day and fasting in Ramadan, they need to avoid socialising in environments where this might be difficult
+ There are nineteen Muslim MPs in the House of Commons, the majority being women (as of 2019)	+ Certain jobs and forms of employment in the West are seen to conflict with Islamic teachings, such as selling alcohol and working in casinos, because alcohol and gambling are prohibited
+ Mosques, halal butchers, Islamic schools and the inclusion of Islam in religious education lessons all benefit Muslims and enable them to participate equally in society	+ Others fear prejudice, Islamophobia or being attacked, as they are abused for being different, for example, by wearing a headscarf
+ Some Muslims feel that wearing Islamic dress, such as hijab, and practising their faith openly, helps integration because others see Muslims and understand more about their religion	+ Some Muslim parents prefer their children to be educated in faith schools and this is not possible in all secular states (although it is possible in others, such as the UK)
+ The Constitution of Madinah, an original model of society for Muslims, is seen by some as a good model for inclusivism and encourages Muslims to live alongside people of other backgrounds	+ Islamic teachings on wealth and finance prevent some Muslims from taking advantage of conventional mortgages and money lending based on an economic system opposed by Islam
+ The Qur'an's teachings, such as about equality between men and women, are shared by the West (see Chapter 9)	+ The need for halal butchers, Islamic banks and Muslim faith schools creates the idea of separation and is thought to prevent Muslims from fully participating in non-Muslim countries
+ Schools and places of work allow Muslims time off for worship and the observance of religious festivals	
+ A BBC Radio 4 *Today* poll found that 95 per cent of Muslims feel loyal to Britain and 93 per cent said they should obey British laws	

Britain's multiculturalism has been seen as a positive way of recognising the distinct identity of different communities. However, there have been concerns that this has enabled some Muslim communities to become detached and distanced from other parts of society, raising questions about their integration into British life. Since the 9/11 attacks in 2001, there has been a rise in Islamophobia, particularly with attacks on women wearing veils and Muslims experiencing prejudice when applying for jobs.

'European Islam'

Integration is seen by many Muslims as a key priority. One idea, proposed by the former Grand Mufti of Bosnia and Herzegovina, Mustafa Ceric, has been to form a 'European Islam'. In his book, *Islam: A Declaration of European Muslims*, Ceric says that a Muslim has both the right and duty to 'carry out his or her noble moral values wherever he or she lives' and this is best achieved through a European imamate (supreme leadership) of the ummah 'as a way of institutionalising Islam in Europe'. He states that this could be achieved by uniting Sunni and Shi'a ideas about leadership into 'one acceptable global Muslim authority' and 'Europe or the West in general, is a good place for such a dream.'

Ceric says that Europe is a 'dār al-sulh (house of social contract)' and also a 'dar al-salam (house of peace)' because Muslims can live in accordance with Islam in European democratic societies as they are 'committed to the rule of law and the protection of the human rights of their citizens who, in turn, must accept the duty to work for the good of the society in an orderly and organised way.' Ceric says that neither Muslims nor Europe are yet mature enough for a single Muslim authority in Europe but this will come eventually because young European Muslims will put their Islamic identity before national or ethnic identities and are 'comfortable with their European identity co-existing with their Islamic upbringing.'

Muslims as a religious minority

+ Similar to Muhammad's hijrah, many Muslims have had to migrate to avoid religious persecution and to find a new and safer life elsewhere, such as in Europe.
+ When significant numbers of Muslims arrived in the UK in the 1950s, one of their first priorities was finding prayer spaces and building mosques. There are said to be approximately 1,700 mosques in Britain which serve not only spiritual but social and other purposes (see Chapter 5).
+ Many Muslims do not see any contradiction in following their faith and playing an active role in wider society, as long as they have freedom of belief, while others prefer to guard their traditions and identity by keeping to their own community.
+ The large majority have maintained religious observances such as the Five Pillars (see Chapter 5) and modest dress, while respecting the law of the land. At the same time, some Muslims attend separate shari`a courts for family matters. These are supported by some under the principle of 'minority jurisprudence' but criticised by other Muslims for unfair treatment of women.
+ Muslim occasions such as Ramadan and Id are supported by members of the royal family, the Prime Minister and other political leaders who read annual messages wishing Muslim communities 'Ramadan Mubarak' and 'Id Mubarak' which makes Muslims feel valued in British society.
+ The government's Prevent strategy has been met with varying responses by Muslims, some being supportive as it seeks to challenge extremism of all forms, while others say it is targeting Muslims.

> **Prevent strategy**
> The UK Government's Prevent strategy aims to safeguard and support those vulnerable to radicalisation, to stop them from becoming terrorists or supporting terrorism

Issues facing a multi-faith society

Western perceptions of Islam

The enormous attention given to Islam and Muslims in the media, in comparison to other religions, has led to negative perceptions of Islam in the West. There is also a tendency to present Islam as a monolith rather than a faith with huge diversity. There is an increasing feeling that there is institutional bias against Islam, leading to misrepresentation.

Political views

An increasing number of Muslims have become politically active and many have been elected to roles in local, regional and national government. Many Muslims serve on local councils and a record number of Muslim MPs were elected in 2019, the majority of these being women. Sadiq Khan, the mayor of London, is another prominent Muslim.

This involvement in politics has not been without challenges. David Cameron's focus on 'British values' rather than multiculturalism and Michael Gove's book *Celsius 7/7*, which argued that a significant proportion of British Muslims hold, or sympathise with, extremist views, have strained relationships between Muslims and those in power. Baroness Sayeeda Warsi highlighted the difficulties for Muslims: 'those who engage with politics or any other British institutions are to be viewed as suspicious, and Muslims who don't engage and keep themselves to themselves are to be treated as suspicious for being separatist and disengaged from mainstream society'. She also called for an investigation into Islamophobia within the Conservative Party of which she is a member.

The question of whether or not Islam is accurately represented in Britain is also debated.

Accurately represented	Inaccurately represented
+ British Muslims hold many influential and leadership positions. + Bodies such as the Muslim Council of Britain (MCB) represents the views of a large number of Muslim institutions to government and in the media	+ Muslims are often viewed with suspicion regardless of whether they strive to become involved in the political process + The MCB often only represents the views of its own affiliates and does not include the views of those who disagree

Media representation

Newspapers

UK tabloids appear fixated with fears about the 'Islamification' of Britain, from shock at burqas and immigration in the *Daily Express*, to outrage about halal meat and poppy-burning in the *Star*. Occasionally the words 'Islamic' and 'Muslim' are used when religion has no relevance to the story, as happened in July 2015 when the *Mail on Sunday* printed a headline 'Muslim gang slashes tyres of immigration-raid van', without any evidence that the perpetrators were Muslim. Similarly, *The Times* newspaper was ruled by the press regulator, the Independent Press Standards Organisation (IPSO), to have distorted a story in August 2017 about a young Christian child being forced into Muslim foster care. Even if apologies and corrections are printed, they are never as prominent as the original story and so the damage is done.

These examples of the treatment of Islam and Muslims help to perpetuate stereotypes about Muslims and have had far-reaching (including violent) effects. Following Boris Johnson's article in the *Telegraph* in which he compared veiled Muslim women to 'letter boxes' and 'bank robbers', Tell MAMA (a national project which records and measures anti-Muslim incidents in the UK) reported that there was a 375 per cent surge in anti-Muslim attacks and instances of abuse.

Television

There are also problems with mainstream TV. Discussion shows about religion, such as the BBC's *The Big Questions*, invite a range of guests to debate topical issues, but have often appeared particularly keen to provide a platform for angry Muslims, perpetuating the stereotype of Muslims as inflexible and quick to take offence.

Documentaries such as ITV's *Islam's Non-believers* (2016), about apostates, have focused on Muslims who believe leaving Islam is a capital offence and given the impression that such a religion cannot be compatible with human rights.

Due to their underrepresentation in the media, many Muslims are now trying to break into the industry. Mishal Husain, Mahdi Hasan and Fatima Manji are notable success stories, but many argue that it isn't the absence of Muslims in top journalistic positions that is the problem; it is a lack of objectivity, fairness and accuracy when reporting on all forms of extremism. When Thomas Mair, the white far-right terrorist who killed the MP Jo Cox, was sentenced to life, the *Daily Mail* published the story on page 30 of that day's edition. Many said that if a Muslim had committed the crime, it would have been front-page news.

At other times, the media has made efforts to represent Muslims. Sitcoms like *Citizen Khan* and *Man Like Mobeen* are aimed at a national audience, despite Muslims being only 5.6 per cent of the population. However, even with Islam as a central theme, their portrayal of British Muslims has led to mixed responses.

Writing in the *Daily Mail* about *Citizen Khan*, Saira Khan expressed relief that there was now 'a home-grown sitcom that allowed British Muslims to laugh at themselves'. She acknowledged that the show dealt with stereotypes but argued that those stereotypes were based in reality. Khan argued that sitcoms like *Citizen Khan* were tools for integration. 'Crucially, if we British Muslims can't laugh at ourselves, with all our cultural tics and traits, and also allow the rest of Britain to laugh at us, too, there's a real danger that our community will end up ostracised and isolated.' MP Rupa Huq, on the other hand, felt that although it was good news that the series had been commissioned, the stereotypes were lazy and unimaginative. '[Citizen Khan is] a lazy comedy that reinforces majority (mis)understanding of Pakistanis/Asians/Muslims.'

Frustrated with so much negativity about their faith, and to cater to the needs of their own communities, Muslims have launched their own newspapers, radio stations, TV channels and news websites. This gives them control over their own content, including what goes in the news and who appears on discussion shows. Examples include *The Muslim News* and Voice of Islam radio.

Muslim groups continue to engage with media outlets and will send press releases to local and national media in order to show their positive contributions to society and demonstrate that Muslims are a fully integrated part of Britain.

The extent to which the media influences Western perception of Islam is debated.

Large influence	Limited influence
+ The age of mass media means news reaches large parts of the population all over the world which influences people to think about Islam in a certain way + Some research, such as that by Ziauddin Sardar, cites many instances of Arabs and Muslims being portrayed in films as barbaric and backward + Bodies like the MCB complain that the media doesn't sufficiently report good works by Muslims and their condemnations of terrorism + The media do not highlight terrorist acts by non-Muslims as much as they do terrorist acts by Muslims	+ Some feel that the media has been too reticent to criticise aspects of Islam and the behaviour of Muslims, in the treatment of women, for example, for fear of backlash + Many documentaries, such as those by the BBC, highlight historical Muslim contributions to science, maths, philosophy and art + Terrorist atrocities are in the news because journalists have a duty to report them, including those which are committed by Muslims

Now test yourself TESTED

7 Write two points supporting the argument that Islam is accurately represented in Britain and two opposing it.

Islamophobia

 REVISED

Sensationalist headlines, media criticism of Islam and the rise of far-right groups such as the English Defence League have led to increasing fears about Muslims. In a survey conducted by HOPE not Hate in 2019, more than a third of Britons agreed that 'Islam is a threat to British life' and another charity, Show Racism the Red Card (SRTRC) found that about a third of 10–16-year-olds agreed or partly agreed that 'Muslims are taking over England' and over a quarter agreed or partly agreed that that 'Islam encourages extremism or terrorism'.

These and other factors have brought the issue of Islamophobia into sharper focus. Islamophobia is a term that first came to prominence in the Runnymede Trust report, 'Islamophobia: A Challenge For Us All' in 1997, in which it was defined as 'an outlook or world-view involving an unfounded dread and dislike of all Muslims, which results in practices of exclusion and discrimination'. In 2019, the All Party Parliamentary Group on British Muslims proposed a new definition of Islamophobia as 'rooted in racism and – a type of racism that targets expressions of Muslimness or perceived Muslimness' but this was rejected by the Government.

Violence against Muslims in other parts of the world has also been seen to embolden anti-Muslim prejudice in the UK. In 2019, a week after a white supremacist killed worshippers at two New Zealand mosques, the number of anti-Muslim hate crimes in the UK increased by 593 per cent.

Muslim Council of Britain

REVISED

The Muslim Council of Britain (MCB) was set up in 1997 as an independent, non-sectarian umbrella body for more than 500 mosques, Muslim organisations, charities and schools from mainly Sunni and Shi'a traditions to 'promote consultation, cooperation and coordination on Muslim affairs in the United Kingdom'. They said it signalled a 'commitment to Muslim unity and pluralism' and provided a foundation for 'respect, dialogue and cooperation among Britain's Muslims'. It encourages Muslims to participate fully in public life and often makes statements on behalf of British Muslims.

Its effectiveness has been both praised and questioned.

Effective	Not effective
✦ The MCB is the broadest based Muslim group in the UK and has succeeded in bringing together a large number of affiliates from different traditions and denominations, who do not always agree with each other ✦ The MCB has joined together with other faith groups at national events, giving a voice and presence for Muslims ✦ The MCB has consistently condemned acts of violence and terrorism in the name of Islam	✦ The MCB has been criticised for some of its affiliates having links to extremist Islamic ideology and its boycott of Holocaust Memorial Day between 2001 and 2007 ✦ During the Iraq war the MCB strayed into international politics and criticised the Government, leading to strained relationships with politicians ✦ The MCB was accused of sectarianism and bigotry towards the Ahmadiyya Muslim community and issued a statement calling them non-Muslims

Interfaith work

 REVISED

Muslims see the diversity of faith, belief and worldviews as a basis for positive interaction, dialogue and enriching society.

Islam's emphasis on respecting and protecting other faiths lays a secure foundation for inter-religious peace. Muslims actively participate in interfaith forums and also join other religious groups in multi-faith action, such as supporting community projects and standing for justice. Many are also involved in projects like the Centre for Muslim-Christian Studies in Oxford whose aims are to 'bring Muslims and Christians together to relate honestly, think rigorously, and explore our respective traditions and religious texts, through teaching and research, discussion and public education'.

Muslims are engaged with the Christian Muslim Forum, Religions for Peace UK and the Inter Faith Network UK. The Qur'an teaches Muslims to find common ground with other faiths and if this is not possible, to still maintain peace (Qur'an 3: 64).

Chapter summary

✦ Madinah at the time of the Prophet Muhammad is believed to be the model state in its religious, moral, social and political structures.

✦ There is no uniformity in Muslim countries about how shari'ah is understood and implemented, and there are varying views about its application in non-Muslim states.

✦ The Qur'an is used to support both exclusivist and inclusivist attitudes to other faiths. Pluralists emphasise Islam's respect, love and tolerance towards followers of different religions and beliefs.

✦ Muslims migrants have struggled to integrate and faced issues in secular and multi-faith societies, and experienced a lot of Islamophobia.

✦ Leading Muslims and Muslim organisations continue to engage in politics and the media to represent Muslim interests, with mixed success.

Exam practice

Analyse different Muslim attitudes to other religious and non-religious worldviews and their truth claims. [Pearson Edexcel, AO1 and AO2, 20]

'Islam is perfectly compatible with democracy.' Evaluate this claim. [Eduqas, AO2, 30]

11 State, society and secularisation

Glossary

Adhan The call to prayer. Page 52

Ahl al-bayt House or family of the Prophet Muhammad. Page 30

Animism Belief that spirits exist in animate and inanimate objects. Page 13

Ascetism Renouncing materialistic things. Page 74

Baqa' Regeneration, permanence or persistence of the self. Page 76

Caliph (Khalifah) successor of the Prophet (Sunni). Page 25

Caliphate System of succession or leadership following the Prophet Muhammad (Sunni). Page 42

Constitution of Madinah An agreement drawn up by the Prophet for the people of Madinah. Page 18

Dhikr The remembrance of Allah, usually associated with Sufis. Page 75

Dhimmis Non-Muslims living in Muslim lands. Page 116

Fana' Self-annihilation or losing one's ego for the sake of Allah. Page 75

Fiqh 'deep understanding' or 'intelligence', later simply known as Muslim jurisprudence or law. Page 23

Hadith Sayings of the Prophet Muhammad. Page 22

Hijrah The journey from Makkah to Madinah by the Prophet and other Muslims in the year 622CE. The Muslim calendar is called the hijri calendar because it begins from this date. Page 18.

Ijma' Agreement by consensus of scholars or the community. Page 22

Ijtihad Interpretative effort or intellectual struggle. Page 22

Imamah Succession or leadership of the Prophet's family (Shi'a). Page 42

Isnad The chain of Hadith reporters. Page 27

Jahiliyya State of ignorance according to Muslims which pre-dated the coming of the Prophet. Page 11

Jihad Striving and struggling in the way of Allah. Page 64

Jinns Spirits or hidden beings. Page 13

Ka`bah Cube-shaped building in Makkah, to which Muslims face while praying. Page 11

Kutubullah Holy books. Page 39

Liberation The state of freedom from any type of oppression or limit on thought and expression. In Islam 'liberation' relates to challenging injustice and bringing about social reform. Page 115

Madhhab School of Muslim law. Page 30

Monotheists Believers in one God. Page 13

Muezzin Muslim who makes the call to prayer. Page 52

Mujtahids Experts in ijtihad. Page 31

Nabi Prophet. Page 38

Night of Power (Laylat al-Qadr) The night the Prophet received his first Qur'anic revelation. Page 16

Niyyah Intention. Page 53

Nubuwwah Prophethood. Page 38

Polytheism Belief in multiple gods. Page 12

Prevent strategy The UK Government's strategy to safeguard and support those vulnerable to radicalisation, to stop them from becoming terrorists or supporting terrorism. Page 121

Qiyas Analogical reasoning. Page 22

Qur'an Muslim sacred text and most important source of authority in Islam. Page 12

Risalah 'Message', referring to belief in Prophets/Messengers of Allah. Page 50

Sahabah Muslims who lived in the time of the Prophet and witnessed his actions. Page 27

Salah Five daily prayers. Page 51

Sawm Fasting. Page 60

Shahadah Declaration of faith. Page 34

Shari`a 'The way to water', referring to the Islamic legal system. Page 22

Shatahat Divinely inspired statements uttered in a state of fana' (Sufi). Page 75

Shirk Setting up partners or equals with Allah. Page 31

Sira An account of the Prophet's life. Page 22

Sunnah Actions of the Prophet. Page 22

Tarawih Additional night prayers in Ramadan (Sunni). Page 61

Tariqas Sufi orders. Page 76

Tawatur The chain of Hadith reports. Page 27

Tawhid Belief in the oneness of Allah. The oneness and unity of Allah. Page 34

Tazkiyat al-nafs Self-purification. Page 75

Ummah Originally, the citizens of Madinah under the Prophet's authority, later evolved to mean the worldwide Muslim community. Page 25

Umrah Lesser pilgrimage to Makkah. Page 19

Urf Local traditions and customs in the time of the Prophet Muhammad. Page 22

Wudu Ritual washing before Salah. Page 51

Suggested answer guidance to exam practice at **www.hoddereducation.co.uk/myrevisionnotesdownloads**

Index

A-level Religious Studies: Islam

Suggested answer guidance to exam practice at **www.hoddereducation.co.uk/myrevisionnotesdownloads**